The Methuen Book of
Contemporary Monologues for Women

Chrys Salt is an award-winning theatre director and writer. She is Artistic Director of 'Bare Boards . . . and a passion' Theatre Company. She now directs extensively in theatre and sound and has worked with many of the country's leading actors. She has written several books including her popular book for actors, *Make Acting Work*, as well as theatre, radio plays and documentaries. She is a regular tutor at the London Actors Centre.

Also available in this series

By Chrys Salt

Making Acting Work

The Methuen Book of Contemporary Monologues for Men

Edited by Annika Bluhm

The Methuen Audition Book for Women

The Methuen Audition Book for Men

Edited by Anne Harvey

The Methuen Book of Monologues for Young Actors

The Methuen Book of Duologues for Young Actors

The Methuen Book of Contemporary Monologues for Women

Edited by
CHRYS SALT

Methuen Drama

Methuen Publishing Limited
215 Vauxhall Bridge Road
London SW1V 1EJ

10 9 8 7 6 5 4 3 2 1

Methuen Publishing Ltd Reg. No. 3543167

A CIP catalogue record for this book is available from the British Library

ISBN 0 413 77291 8

Typeset by SX Composing DTP, Rayleigh, Essex
Printed and bound in Great Britain by
Cox and Wyman Ltd, Reading, Berkshire

Caution

Disclaimer

The editor and publisher gratefully acknowledge permission to reproduce the
quoted extracts within this work. Every effort has been made to trace the
copyright holders of the extracts included in this work. The publishers apologise
for any unintended omissions and would be most grateful for any information
that would enable them to amend any omissions in future editions.

Contents

Introduction

This book aims to direct you towards an audition piece that is not only right for you, but right for the audition in hand so you can bring your unique qualities to the character you have chosen.

When you are called to audition, you will either be asked to read a chunk of text 'cold' as in: 'She's a Lithuanian pole vaulter with a penchant for beer . . . would you mind reading it for me?' or to perform something from your audition repertoire. You'll certainly need a handful of pieces under your belt whether it's the usual 'one classical and one contemporary' for drama school entry or something prepared for a specific audition for theatre, fringe or even an agent.

In any event, it's valuable experience to research a play and perform a speech – even if it has no immediate purpose. It keeps your mind alive and your creative juices flowing.

When you are choosing your audition piece, think carefully what suits you and what you are auditioning *for*. No good wheeling out your deathless Antigone for Theatre in Education (TIE) or that Victoria Wood monologue for the latest Anthony Neilson play. Nor should you render your Juliet if you are fully forty-two and look like an escapee from *EastEnders*. Be sensible.

When I was writing my book, *Make Acting Work*, I had an interesting chat with Jude Kelly (former artistic director of the West Yorkshire Playhouse). I'll quote it again because you might like to bear what she says in mind when deciding which audition piece to choose:

> It's very hard to make actors understand that you are often not turning them down because they are less good than somebody else – you turn them down because they are not . . . right in some way. Actors get very upset about this and yet if you ask them what they think of such and such a production, they often say, 'So and so was completely wrong for that part.' At the same time they will be arguing for a completely level playing field without any version of 'typecasting' at all . . .

Your task at audition is not only to show that you might be right for *this particular job*, but that you are an artist with talent and imagination – so even if you are not 'right' this time round you will certainly stick in my mind when a casting director is looking for a similar role. Remember casting personnel probably don't have a file for 'good actor'. How could they keep track? But they might have one for 'glamorous granny', 'sexy blonde' or 'tough professional'. They'll want to keep you on file if your work has impressed.

Some parts fit like thermal underpants. They are comfortable, snug and they belong to you. Something inside you keys into the character's soul. The feelings she expresses, the language she uses. Her class. Her agenda. It just feels 'right'. The text comes 'trippingly off the tongue'. You have the right physical equipment. These are the pieces to go for. You may be wearing them for some time, so make sure they fit.

An audition piece should be a little artefact in its own right. Sometimes (heresy oh heresy) you won't need to read the play. Taken out of context you can make it your own. I recently snaffled a piece from an old Emlyn Williams play, *The Corn is Green* (set in a Welsh mining community). Out of context, with a bit of tinkering and an alternative 'back story', it worked well for an Irish actor with a line in IRA terrorists. (Sorry, Emlyn!)

On most occasions, however, it's *vital* to read the play. And don't read it once, read it several times. There's an apocryphal story about the actor who goes into the radio studio to read *A Book at Bedtime*. He hasn't read the book and thinks he can wing it. It is only when he gets deep into Chapter 1 and reads 'said Stephen with his customary lisp' . . . He hadn't done his homework, so do yours.

A couple of minutes is a short space of time for you to 'strut your stuff' so here are a few tips I hope you will find helpful. Bear them in mind in conjunction with the commentaries I have written when you are doing your study.

- Find out every last thing you can about your character and her journey. Look at the writer's stage directions. They will give you valuable clues. Then there are things that you will have to find out for yourself. What do other people have to say about her? What has happened to her? What drives her? What does she want? Where has she come from? Where is she now? Church? Park? Drawing room? Arctic waste? Sauna? Who is she talking to? What's their relationship? Why is she saying this now? What is the style? What's the period? What does she do for a living? What's she wearing? Crinoline? Stilettos? Trainers? Everything makes a difference. It's 1902. Did women cross their legs? Rigour is the name of the game. Play the situation. Play the intention. The text is just icing on the cake. If I say 'You have lovely blue eyes' am I making an observation, admiring your physical attributes or telling you I love you? How many other things could it mean? Try it using a different subtext each time. You'll see what I mean.

- Never watch yourself in the mirror or listen to yourself on tape. You'll end up trying to reproduce that magic gesture or meaningful inflection. Unless you engage with the character afresh each time, your audition piece will become a stilted, stale affair – all form and no content. Practise your pieces regularly so you are not caught on the hop when the phone rings.

- Don't let nerves carry you off. Fear is the enemy and will spoil all that beautiful work you did in the bedroom. If you don't get this job, you won't lose a leg. Get your audition in perspective. Remember, if I've asked to see you, I *want* you to be good. It would be such a relief to cast this part, fill this course or take you on as a client. Do me a favour and give yourself a chance. Take some time before you begin. Close your eyes for a few moments. I'm happy to wait for your good work. Breathe deeply. Engage with your character. Exclude the paraphernalia of the audition situation from your thinking. You are no longer in a cluttered office at Television Centre or facing a battalion of watchful faces. You are in nineteenth-century France. Or facing the child you gave away twenty years ago. You are not here to show how clever you are. You are not *showing*, you are *being*. You are here to bring two minutes of your character's life into my room. The ground under your feet is the ground she walks on. You have slipped into her skin. You wear her life. You have transformed.

3

- Wear something you feel comfortable in. Those biting new shoes will distract you from the job in hand. Dress appropriately. Foolish to wear your décolletage for that solicitor, or those stilettos for Lady Anne.
- Keep your hair out of your face. I need to see your eyes. They really are the mirrors of the soul. If you are *thinking* it right, it will *be* right. It won't matter to me how brilliantly you can mime drowning in a vat of porridge, if your work doesn't have the ring of truth about it, I won't be interested.

So it's over to you. My commentaries should not be seen as 'giving direction' in anything but the loosest sense. But I have tried to give a few tips and indicators about context and approach, point you towards a few clues buried in the language or the syntax.

The pieces are arranged in an 'age ladder' – the youngsters at the beginning – so I hope that will make it easy for you to locate an appropriate piece. Sometimes, of course, a character's age is flexible and can be adapted to work for you so I have avoided being too specific. I have left in stage directions where they seem relevant, and on the odd occasion, slightly tinkered with the text (where indicated) so it works better out of context. I hope you'll find this useful.

May the creative force be with you. Good luck.

This book is dedicated to all my students and friends in the profession from whom I learn so much.

Thanks are due to Elizabeth Ingrams, my editor at Methuen, for her good humour, unflappable support and insightful blue pencil and to Richard, my husband, for his TLC, cups of tea and inexhaustible supply of ink cartridges.

Dreams of Anne Frank *by Bernard Kops*

Dreams of Anne Frank is the story of an extraordinary thirteen-year-old Jewish girl who went into hiding with her family after the Nazi occupation of Holland. Although based on the real-life *Diary of Anne Frank*, Bernard Kops's play is an imaginative exploration of Anne's thoughts and dreams. Through these she can escape, travel, prophesy and even change the course of history!

I have created this monologue by linking several speeches from the beginning of the play together. Anne is an impulsive, creative, impressionable adolescent who dreams of becoming a writer. Her diary, given to her on her thirteenth birthday, is her most treasured possession.

In the first part of the speech, Anne tells of the yellow Star of David, a badge that all Jews were required to wear. She catalogues the restrictions placed on Jews and tells how quickly life changed under German occupation. She delivers this, almost like a shopping list – its emotional punch packed in the practical unemotional delivery. Take care not to colour this section with hindsight – things you would know, but she would not. The bald facts are shocking in their own right.

In the next section Anne describes the morning when Anne's father, Otto, announces the family must go into hiding. Despite Otto's attempts to normalise the event for his children, Anne senses something momentous is happening. Her mind is in turmoil. When and where are they going? Will they be all right? Conflicting emotions chase each other round Anne's head. She's sad to leave her house, but happy to escape the Germans. Excited to be packing up her things, but what does the future hold? Look at the 'essentials' she chooses to take with her. School books and Hollywood pin-ups. Pencils and perfume – this is an adolescent on the cusp of womanhood not the virtuous victim of popular preconception. How much does she really understand of what lies ahead?

In the end it is Anne's diary that offers consolation and escape. It will be her hope and friend through the dark times ahead. As her diary says, 'Even if you are locked away, everything is possible in your head!'

Anne (*holding up a yellow star*) Morning star. Evening star. Yellow star, Amsterdam. Nineteen forty-two. The German army occupies Holland. They have applied terrible rules that we must obey. Rules for Jews. That applies to me. 'Jews must wear a yellow star. Jews cannot go on trains. Jews must not drive. Jews cannot go shopping, except between three and five. Jews must only patronize Jewish shops.' We cannot go to the cinema, play tennis, go swimming. I cannot even go to the theatre. And now for the most frightening thing of all. They are beginning to round Jews up and take us away. Away from our homes, our beloved Amsterdam. A few days ago I celebrated my thirteenth birthday. My parents gave me this diary. It is my most precious possession. Yesterday I was just an ordinary girl living in Amsterdam. Today I am forced to wear this by our Nazi conquerors. Morning start, evening star, yellow star.

It was Sunday. The fifth of July. The day after American Independence Day. My mother pretended she wasn't crying.

Then Father made the announcement. I remember his exact words. 'Listen, children. Please. I must tell you something. We're going into hiding.' When are we going into hiding? Will we be all right? What do I leave behind? What can I take? (*Getting her satchel.*) Essentials. My school satchel. I'm going to cram it full. Hair curlers. Handkerchiefs. School books. Film star photographs. Joan Crawford. Bette Davis. Deanna Durbin. Mickey Rooney. Comb. Letters. Thousands of pencils. Elastic bands. My best book. *Emil and the Detectives*. Five pens. (*She smells a little bottle.*) Nice scent. Oh yes! Mustn't forget my new diary. (*She has put all her things into her satchel but she has not included her diary.*) We're going into hiding. Going into hiding.

Four days later. It was Thursday, the ninth of July. I shall never forget that morning. It was raining. Imagine leaving your house, maybe for ever.

I'm so happy. In hiding we no longer have to obey the Germans, the master race. No more dreaded rules for Jews.

Goodbye, House. We'll always remember you. Thank you for everything. My brain is at a fairground, on the roller coaster. Up and down. Happy. Sad. Afraid. Excited. My emotions are racing. My imagination spilling over. After all, I am a creative artist. I'm going to be a writer when this war is over.

Diary! Can't go without my diary. (*She takes up the diary and opens it.*) You can be trapped in a box, or in sadness, but you travel in your mind. You can be imprisoned in a basement or an attic, but you can go anywhere. In your dreams you are free, the past, the present, the future. It is all open to you within my pages. Use me well. (*As herself.*) I promise. I shall write everything down. Everything. Thoughts. Events. Dreams. I shall confide my secrets. Only to you. (*Clutching her diary close.*) Let's go. My diary. I couldn't survive without my diary.

Cooking with Elvis *by Lee Hall*

Jill is fourteen – an unhappy overweight adolescent. She's working-class and from the North. Here she talks to Dad, an erstwhile Elvis impersonator, who is in a vegetative state and wheelchair-bound as a result of a traffic accident.

Jill has every reason to be miserable. Mum's carping criticism, neglect and preoccupation with 'getting laid' coupled with Dad's invalidity leave her feeling abandoned. Unloved and unlovely. Why is she always the one 'left alone in her bedroom', the one 'nobody fancies', the one 'with the hideous hair band'? She sublimates her misery in cooking, which becomes a driving mission.

Look at the lavishness of the imagery, the succulence of the language. If 'Food is love', what might these images denote? If Dad can't speak or hear her, she can safely reveal her deepest feelings, can't she? What do these descriptions of culinary delights, indulgence and physical abandonment say about her? The succulent world she invents, the unlikely 'country kitchen' future she dreams of, stand in sharp contrast to real life. A domestic idyll. If she can imagine it big enough and wish for it hard enough, maybe it will come true. Interesting that in her imaginary world Dad is still there – fed and watered but hidden away 'in the back'.

Her final unanswerable question, 'and then we'd be happy. Wouldn't we? Wouldn't we?' is a moving appeal to the dad she has lost, expressing a desperate yearning for love, happiness and for life to be otherwise.

———————————

Jill Scene Twelve. A speech about cooking. In the olden days they used to think that cooking was something special. Mark Antony once gave his cook a whole city cos Cleopatra liked his gravy. Those were the days when they really appreciated things. They went all over the world to get stuff to eat. Fantastic ingredients from all over the world. Camels' feet cooked in roses. Whole plates of nightingales' tongues, pigs that when you carved them doves would fly out, marinaded lentils wrapped in gold. You see, they appreciated food and it was good to be fat. It was sexy to be fat. When you see them old paintings of women in the nude – they weren't skinny, were they? They had something to be proud of. Big pink tummies, enormous soft thighs and they were always stuffing themselves with a bunch of grapes. Sometimes I have this dream, where I'm lying there in the middle of an enormous bowl of fruit, and I'm lying there in the kiwis and papayas, totally naked, eating chocolate puddings. I suppose, in that way, I'm quite old-fashioned, really. And when I grow up that's what I want to be, Dad. A cook and I'd have a husband who was a gourmet and we'd live in a little cottage with hams hanging from the rafters and every day we'd make the most exquisite recipes known to man. And you'd be there too. In the back. And we'd pass your stuff through a little hatch in the wall. Delicious delicacies that we'd pass through to your bit. And then we'd be happy, Dad. Wouldn't we? Wouldn't we?

Tokens of Affection *by Maureen Lawrence*

Liane is an emotionally deprived adolescent from a disadvantaged background. She has been committed to a unit for female juvenile offenders for refusing to go to school, but is out of place amongst the other violent inmates, whose challenging behaviour is almost impossible to contain. Liane is archetypal victim material – physically small, frightened, needy, easily-led with low self-esteem and poor personal hygiene. She is mistreated, battered and unwanted by her mum at home and bullied and abused by inmates in the unit. She is isolated and in desperate need of love.

At this point, Liane's chief abuser, Debbie, has been 'on the run' after a row with staff. Her absence has left the unit a calmer and more constructive place and given Liane some peace. A new member of staff, sympathetic and more understanding of the girl's needs, has just begun to turn things around when Debbie comes back to throw things into disarray.

Consider Liane's state of mind as she delivers this speech. She has just been in a fight with Debbie over Kelly, who has briefly been her friend while Debbie was away. As Liane sees it, Debbie's agenda is to reclaim Kelly's allegiance and her position as 'top dog' in the unit leaving her once more 'out in the cold'. She has just witnessed the new girl Andrea – who hasn't spoken a word since her arrival at the unit – vandalising Kelly's precious sewing with a craft knife. Andrea is discovered, still holding the knife, when Liane enters at the beginning of the speech. What trips Liane's switch? The stage direction says 'involuntarily'. (Always look at stage directions. They often give you vital clues.) Does she see Andrea's destruction of Kelly's sewing as an act of silent solidarity? The speech seems to come completely out of the blue. Liane presents herself as tough and unaffected by events but it is a 'front'. The brutality and neglect of her brief history speak for themselves. She reaches out to Andrea who she instinctively knows is as lonely and miserable as she is.

12

Liane (*involuntarily*) Debbie nicked that knife off Mrs Leiver. It goes in the cupboard. Now she's come, she'll try and get Kelly back. I'll be on my own again. I never had a mate of my own. Even at home. They all pick on me. It's because I look like my dad. When they sent me away to that school, my mother never meant for me to come back. She burned my bed. She took it out into the yard and burned everything. You can see where she did it – the bits that wouldn't burn just got left there. I said: you expect me to fucking sleep in the yard on a bunch of burnt rags and she hit me across the mouth. I don't care. I lie on the sofa and watch telly all night till it wakes me up with that whining it makes. (*Pause.*) Debbie won't touch you: you're big. You've got brothers. Do you talk to your brothers? My mam gets like, paralysed. Stiff as a board. We have to lug her on to the lavatory, me and our June. It was all right here without Debbie. Better than stopping in the house. Are you miserable? Why don't you say nothing? My mother says I never stop yapping. How do you stop yourself yapping? My mother says she's going to put tape on my lips. Andrea? It's miles better here than at school. I'm never going back to no school. If them in schools knew what it was like when you get expelled they'd all be getting expelled. Schools would be empty. Teachers would be out of work. You won't get me nowhere near. You think when you hear that word expelled it means something terrible, but it's a big con. Me, first of all I had a holiday for seven weeks and then I ended up in this place. Our June, that's my sister, the one that's pregnant, our June says: trust you to fall on your feet. My mother says: better to fall on your feet, our June, than flat on your back with your legs wide open. Andrea? Can you hear me? If Debbie gets Kelly back, you could ask Mrs Rushworth if you could be with me? Andrea?

Beached *by Kevin Hood*

Maria is about seventeen. She is small, smart, streetwise and working-class with little sense of self-worth. She's a window-dresser. Although her parents are Italian, she was born and raised in her father's chip shop in Catford and speaks in that vernacular. Her father, Giovanni, abused and neglected her. Her mother deserted her when she was a baby. She is on the run with Peter, another damaged teenager from her neighbourhood. He has brought her to the deserted beach of a bird sanctuary where they are camping out. She is cold, hungry and upset because Peter has rejected her sexual advances.

Both Maria and Peter have good reasons for leaving Catford. Maria wants to escape life in the chip shop and find her mother. For Peter the sanctuary is a safe haven, remembered from a school trip – a place to escape a painful home life. His mother, a prostitute, has kicked him out. Maria set him up to rob her father's shop so she can go to Canada and find her mother. But Giovanni discovers Peter in the shop and comes at him with a knife. In the ensuing struggle, Giovanni is stabbed. Robbery has turned, possibly, to murder. Peter is horrified, but Maria isn't concerned. She hates her father, and with good reason.

Maria often begins with 'I'll tell you a story' as if this distances her from events. And it's a shocking story. Locked up to protect her virginity. A squalid gang rape in the back of a van. But there is no self-pity in the telling. Maria has barricaded herself against emotion. The tone of the speech is defiant in the face of pain remembered. But the silence and pauses in the middle of the speech suggest she is not as hard-boiled as she makes out. Maria has learnt not to expect much out of life. 'What's wrong with me?' she sobs when Peter rejects her. It's a rejection that confirms her low opinion of herself. Under the story is the road map to the angry, damaged person she is now.

Maria has run away to try and salvage something of her sorry life but finds an emotional dead-end on the edge of the land. 'Beached' and stranded in more ways than one.

Maria I'll tell you a story, shall I? 'Bout when I was younger. Thirteen. And 'im, on 'is own with me. Me growin' up, 'im wonderin' 'ow I'm goin' to turn out. Well . . . every time 'e goes down the pub, 'e locks me in. With me chocolate and me crisps and the portable telly. And at first I can't work it out. And then it dawns. (*Pause.*) What 'e thinks is, first fella I see – I'm on me back with me legs wide open, waitin' for it. That's what 'e thinks. I don't like that. I ain't 'avin' that. So . . . one night, one Monday night I'm out the winder and leggin' it down Lewisham with some of the naughty girls from school. Disco. (*Pause.*) I mean, what did I expect, eh? Moonlight in me Chianti? Candlelight on me chips? Well, what I got was warm lager, lots and lots of warm lager, and these three fellas, this band, in the back of their van . . . one after the other.

Silence.

Didn't know what was 'appenin'. Thirteen and pissed, see. (*Pause.*) Long walk 'ome, I tell ya. (*Pause.*) But . . . by the time 'e's openin' the front door there I am, tucked up in bed, all safe and sound. With this 'andful of J-Cloths and ice between my legs. And prayin', oh sweet Maria, prayin' I can 'old off cryin' long enough, 'cause every particle tells me if 'e finds out, 'e's goin' to kill me, I mean really kill me. But it's *all right*. Door opens. 'Buona notte, Mariucca.' Papa . . . and I almost cry, I almost . . . the thing that saves me is the smell on 'im, beer. That smell. Them fellas. 'Im. (*Pause.*) That was the last of 'im for me. No, Peter, I ain't worried about Giovanni.

Joyriders *by Christina Reid*

Sandra is aged around seventeen. She is Northern Irish, tough, cynical and intelligent – a Catholic, raised on the notorious Divis Flats Estate in Belfast (reputedly one of the most disadvantaged housing estates in Western Europe). The play is set at the height of the sectarian violence of the 1980s.

Sandra is on a youth training programme, set up in a disused textile mill for young offenders who are either on probation or suspended sentence for petty crime or joyriding.

Arthur, another trainee, accidentally scarred and disabled by a British Army bullet, has been awarded £70,000 compensation for his injuries. Arthur dreams, somewhat unrealistically, of opening a posh restaurant in Belfast and has just asked Sandra to marry him and be his business partner. Sandra turns down his proposal flat. As far as she's concerned it's a pipe dream programmed for failure, like everything else. Sandra has no illusions about what life has in store for her and her kind. It is defined in terms of what she can't have rather than what she can. A world of 'them and us'. Everything she sees around her confirms her view.

Sandra's single experience of joyriding was an empowering event when for once that 'posh' was within her sights. The fact that the car ran out of petrol and she had to walk home typifies her experience of life. So she's having none of Arthur's proposal. She knows where that road leads. She wants to be in the driving seat of her life – not subjugated by the drudgery of marriage and children like her mother – quite a subversive position for a woman of her age and class to take.

The way Sandra survives her circumstances is to erect a wall of cynicism – believe in nothing and aspire to nothing – that way she won't be disappointed.

Sandra The one an' only time I ever wore a white lace frock, Arthur, was for my first communion . . . an' my mother parades me down the road to get my photo tuk, an' she says to the photographer, 'Isn't our Sandra a picture? Won't she make a beautiful bride?' an' I told her I was never gonna get married, an' she got all dewy-eyed because she thought I wanted to be a nun . . . A bride of Christ, or forty years' hard labour . . . my mother thinks anything in between is a mortal sin . . . She married a big child like you, Arthur, an' what did it get her . . . eight kids an' twenty years' cookin', cleanin' an' survivin' on grants an' handouts . . . You're too like my da fer comfort. Fulla big plans that'll come to nuthin' because yer too soft an' yer too easy-goin' an havin' all that money won't make ye any different. Whatever your da an' the rest of your ones don't steal from ye, the world will. They'll ate ye alive . . . You know what the big trick in this life is? It's knowin' what ye don't want, an' I don't want to be a backseat joyrider, content to sit and giggle behind the fellas who do the stealin' an' the drivin' . . . I stole a car once . . . all by myself . . . I never told nobody, doin' it was enough . . . I just drove it roun' them posh streets in south Belfast until it ran outa petrol, an' then I walked home. Didn't need to boast about it the way the fellas do . . . just doin' it was enough . . . When the careers' officer come to our school, he asked me what I wanted to do, an' I says, 'I wanna drive roun' in a big car like yer woman outa *Bonnie an' Clyde*, an, rob banks,' an' he thought I was takin' a hand out him, so I says, 'All right then, I'll settle for bein' a racin' driver.' An' he says, 'I'd advise you to settle for something less fantastic, Sandra.' . . . They're all the same. They ask ye what ye wanta be, an' then they tell ye what yer allowed to be . . . Me wantin' to be a racin' driver is not more fantastical than Maureen believin' the fairy stories . . . dilly daydream, just like her mother before her . . . somewhere over the rainbow, bluebirds die . . .

Colored Girls Who Have Considered Suicide When the Rainbow is Enuf *by Ntozake Shange*

This is a collection of poems by African-American writer/performer Ntozake Shange which come together to make a single statement about black girls growing up. Shange calls it a choreopoem. She uses poetry, music and dance to distil experiences common to women – loss of virginity, rape, abortion, prejudice and failed relationships. It is a piece that explores the realities of seven different kinds of women who are named only after the colours they are wearing. You can dip into it for audition pieces at will.

Lady in Yellow, in the section I have chosen, is aged about eighteen. It is graduation night in Mercer County. She and a group of young black boys have just graduated and head off to celebrate and party with friends. They set off into their new grown-up lives in a deep black Buick (evocatively described as 'smellin of thunderbird and ladies on heat'), drive like the clappers and drop into a high-octane party where Lady in Yellow dances with provocative hip-swivelling abandon. Finally she escapes to the warm back seat of the car to lose her virginity to Bobby, a seventh grade sweetheart. Mission accomplished.

Notice how Shange avoids punctuation, setting out the text in a 'free verse' format, using capital letters to achieve emphasis and the odd forward slash to indicate a hiatus in the exuberant drive of the language. The kids are American but Lady in Yellow speaks in the cadence and idiom of Shange's African heritage.

This is Lady in Yellow's rite of passage from 'mama to whatever was out there' culminating in her triumphal cry, 'WE WAZ GROWN. WE WAZ FINALLY GROWN.'

The thrill for the actor is to engage with the joyful lyricism of Shange's poetry. The piece has a wonderful circularity about it. Evoke the imagery for us – the pace, the sexual energy of youngsters, free and out 'on the town'.

Lady in Yellow

it was graduation nite & i waz the only virgin in the crowd
bobby mills martin jerome & sammy yates eddie jones & randi
all cousins
all the prettiest niggers in this factory town
carried me out wit em
in a deep black buick
smellin of thunderbird & ladies in heat
we rambled from camden to mount holly
laughin at the afternoon's speeches
& danglin our tassles from the rear-view mirror
climbin different sorta project stairs
movin toward snappin beer cans &
GET IT GET IT THAT'S THE WAY TO DO IT MAMA
all mercer county graduated the same nite
    cosmetology secretarial pre-college autoshop & business
all us movin from mama to whatever waz out there

that nite we raced a big ol truck from the barbeque stand
trying to tell him bout the party at jacqui's
where folks graduated last year waz waitin to hit it wid us
i got drunk & cdnt figure out
whose hand waz on my thigh/but it didn't matter
cuz these cousins martin eddie sammy jerome & bobby
waz my sweethearts alternately since the seventh grade
& everybody knew i always started cryin if somebody actually
tried to take advantage of me
    at jacqui's
ulinda mason was stickin her mouth all out
while we tumbled out the buick
eddie jones waz her lickin stick
but i knew how to dance
    it got soo hot
vincent ramos puked all in the punch
& harly jumped all in tico's face

cuz he was leavin for the navy in the mornin
hadda kick ass so we'd all remember how bad he waz
seems like sheila & marguerite waz fraid
to get their hair turnin back
so they laid up against the wall
lookin almost sexy
didnt wanna sweat
but me & my fellas   we waz dancin

since 1963 i'd won all kinda contests
wid the cousins at the POLICE ATHLETIC LEAGUE DANCES
all mercer county knew
any kin to martin yates cd turn somersaults
fore smokey robinson cd get a woman excited
we danced   doin nasty ol tricks
doin nasty ol tricks I'd been thinkin since may
cuz graduation nite had to be hot
& i waz the only virgin
so i hadda make like my hips waz inta some business
that way everybody thot whoever was gettin it
was a older man cdnt run the streets wit youngsters
martin slipped his leg round my thigh
the dells bumped 'stay'
up & down – up & down the new carver homes
WE WAZ GROWN   WE WAZ FINALLY GROWN

bobby whispered i shd go wit him
fore they go ta cuttin
fore the police arrived
we teetered silently thru the parkin lot
no un uhuh
we didn't know nothing bout no party
bobby started lookin at me
yeah

he started looking at me real strange
like i waz a woman or somethin
started talkin real soft
in the back seat of that ol buick
WOW
by daybreak
i just cdnt stop grinnin.

Her Aching Heart *by Bryony Lavery*

Molly is a young girl from a village in Cornwall – a character in a Gothic romance about the ill-fated love between her and the rich, feisty heroine, Lady Harriet Helstone, mistress of baronial Helstone Hall.

Bryony Lavery uses an entertaining parody of romantic fiction (shades of Charlotte Brontë and Georgette Heyer) to explore issues of class, gender, sexuality and lesbian passion – but this is the writer's agenda, not the actor's. You cannot play parody, only the character's situation.

Here, Molly and Lady Harriet have parted for ever but Molly recounts her dream of returning to Helstone Hall – scene of happier times. Molly, now a votive nun, has honoured her pact with the Almighty to dedicate her life to His service if He delivers her beloved Harriet from the guillotine. In the spirit of the genre, the prose is 'high', larded with adjectives, dense with clichés and as baroque as a Hammer Horror movie.

But the comedy and the pathos are in Molly's love and yearning for Harriet and her efforts to make her story sound 'literary' and vivid. If you feel any temptation to overplay the text, resist it. Consider rather how you might pace it to reflect the pace and atmosphere of Molly's physical and emotional journey from the desolation of the locked gates, across the choked grounds, to the heart of the house which once was full of life and Harriet.

A Cornish accent will mitigate the purple prose, which the playwright cheerfully acknowledges is 'a cornucopia of romantic gush'.

A woman enters, dressed in a shift. Her heart is aching. Anguish clouds her sweet eyes.

Molly Last night I dreamt I went to Helstone Hall again. It seemed to me I stood before the intricately wrought-iron gate leading to the densely wooded drive, and for a while I could not enter for the way was barred to me. There was a lock and chain keeping shut the gate. I called in my dream to the lodge-keeper . . . crusty, kindly Samuel, 'Helloooo! Let me by!' But no answer came and peering through the rusted rococo I saw that Samuel's cheery cottage was empty. No smoke curled from the chimney. No smell of baking bread issued from the gaping door. No comfort met me.

Then, like all dreamers, I was possessed of a sudden with supernatural powers . . . and I passed like a spirit through the gate and was racing, like a thing possessed, up the twisting drive. Past the gnarled oaks choked with ivy. Past the rhododendron bushes twisted and tortured. Past the bracken rank and wild. And I stood before the mighty, looming presence of Helstone Hall.

She clutches at her heart.

Ooooooh! Dear Watcher, it was EMPTY!!!!!! The Great Lawn, once smooth and green as a billiard table . . . was tossed and torn with mole-mounds . . . The soaring grey-granite walls were choked and poked with thrusting tendrils of ivy . . . The mullioned windows, once twinkling with bubbled bright glass, were broken, dark . . . like blinded eyes. Helstone Hall was an empty shell, just as is now my breast where once beat my gentle heart.

Her tears flow, like the River Dart, fast and furious. She picks up a black garment, wipes her eyes upon it. She puts it on.

Moonlight can play odd tricks upon the fancy . . . for in my dream, excitement rippled through my slight form . . . and I could swear the house was not empty . . . but pulsed with life . . . Pungent woodsmoke puffed from the myriad chimney pots, warm light from many-branched silver candlesticks streamed from the windows and the warm night air carried the sound of human voices.

The wild and extravagant Helstones down from London with their rakish friends . . . the rich and dissolute men (*She puts on a white close-fitting hood.*), the beautiful powdered women (*She puts on a cross.*) and at the centre of that glittering throng rich and lovely, ardent and wilful, the impetuous Lady Harriet Helstone. (*She puts on a wimple.*) Harriet. (*With warm affection.*) Harriet. (*With lust.*) Harriet. (*With longing.*) Harriet. (*With hatred.*) Harriet. (*With emptiness.*) Harriet.

She picks up a Bible and exits.

Bloody Poetry *by Howard Brenton*

In 1816 the poets Byron and Shelley met for the first time on the banks of Lake Geneva. *Bloody Poetry* is about the relationship between them and their women, Harriet Westbrook, Mary Shelley (née Godwin) and Claire Clairmont.

Harriet Westbrook was Shelley's first wife. This is almost her only appearance in the play (although she does appear briefly as a ghost) so she is not described in any detail. Your characterisation need not be hampered by fact as there is not a great deal of historical information about Harriet's life.

Shelley eloped with Harriet when she was just sixteen, but the marriage was doomed to failure. Harriet was, by all accounts, beautiful, amiable, accommodating, adequately educated and well bred, but she was not Shelley's intellectual or social equal and he soon tired of her, abandoning her for Mary Godwin when she was pregnant with their second child.

At this point in the play Harriet is pregnant again by an army officer who has been posted to India, leaving her alone and destitute. She is about to commit suicide by jumping into the Serpentine.

This is a complex speech full of contrasts in tone and pace. Is she drunk? Crazed by misery and loss? The speech speaks in dramatic shorthand of the distance she has fallen since Shelley's abandonment. Splenetic outbursts of doggerel and jibing rhymes counterpoint Shelley's lyrical stanzas, which Harriet colours with her feelings of anger and desperation. Shelley's poetry – when not in quotation marks – is distinguished by its rhyme and metre and stands in sharp contrast to Harriet's ramblings. One minute she's 'playing the whore', the next, spitting out Shelley's poetry, scorning it as vapid posturing until finally, shifting into the literary tones of her suicide note, there is a glimpse the woman Shelley first fell in love with. This is a mind in disarray driven mad by the effect of an artist's love and betrayal. The 'hummed screams' should come from a deep and terrible place.

At the time of her tragic suicide Harriet Westbrook was just twenty-one.

Harriet

I married a poet. Fine poet, was he –
name o' Percy Bysshe Shel-ley!

She giggles then backs away, frightened.

Men in the trees.

She calls out.

Shillin'? Shillin'? Want me for a shillin'?

Low.

Men in the trees, midnight London, Hyde Park, banks of the
Serpentine. I am most refined, *most* refined, yer want me fer a
shillin'? Go down all fours on a grass? Or shall I recite tastefully,
verse he did write for me?

'Whose eyes have I gazed fondly on,
And loved mankind the more?
Harriet! On thine: – thou wert my purer mind;
Thou wert the inspiration of my song' –

Tinkly stuff, in't it, dear, rather my arse fer a shillin', dear? I was but
sixteen when I married the poet, sir, where is he now? 'E is on the
continent, sir, on the Con-ti-nont! With sweet Mary, Mare-ree! Who
calls herself his wife, though she not be, I be, legal-ly. Though she
be, intellectually, my superior.

A hummed scream.

Mmmmmmmmmmmmmmmmmmmmmm –

Now I live with a solider name o' Smith, but he has gone to India,
and I call me Harriet Smith – that none may know I was had by the
poet Shel-ly –

Cruel-ly –

Mmmmmmmmmmmmmmmmmmmmmm –

Spitting the lines out.

Who telleth a tale of unending death?
Who lifteth the veil of what is to come?
Who painteth the shadows that are beneath
The wide-winding caves of the peopled tomb?
Or untieth the hopes of what shall be
With the fears and the love for which we see?

Pretty, pretty clever boy, Bysshe!
Ti-tum-ti-tum about death!

All that we know, or feel, or see,
Shall pass like an unreal mystery!

She blows a raspberry.

Yer want t'know 'bout death, mister poet, you go whorin' fer a
shillin' in midnight London!

Dialect change again, quoting her suicide note.

My dear Bysshe, let me conjure you up by the remembrance of our
days of happiness – I could never refuse you and if you had never
left me I have might have lived – but as it is I freely forgive you and
may you enjoy that happiness that you have deprived me of – now
comes the sad task of saying farewell –

She giggles.

Now I'll go for a swim, go for a swim, like a little girl, by the sea-
shore – wash off the men, swim. I . . .

She drowns.

Can't Stand Up for Falling Down
by Richard Cameron

This play is set in a coal-mining town on a stretch of the River Don in the writer's native South Yorkshire. It is about three young women, all deeply affected by the senseless death of a local man; all with good reason to hate the heartless town bully, Royce Boland.

The story unfolds through a cross-hatching of their partial perspectives and a series of intersecting monologues, which are often, like this one, addressed directly to the audience.

Lynette is a working-class Yorkshire lass of twenty-two. She married Royce at eighteen but has lived to regret it. She was brought up to believe marriage is sacred and you must try your hardest to make it work. But Royce is a violent drunkard who beats, demeans and terrorises her. There is not much to Lynette's life. She is old before her time. Royce has forced her to give up her job in the coal board offices. She cleans. She cooks. Sometimes she works in their fishing tackle shop. Sometimes, to get away, she goes down to the river, where she has memories of childhood happiness. But although she has been brutalised and humiliated there is still enough spark in her to answer back. There are even flashes of a bleak sense of humour. She wants to leave but has nowhere else to go – and there are some moments where he is sorry and things improve for a while. As she fixes the bedroom lock to keep Royce at bay, he is in the shed making a go-kart for his seven-year-old son by another woman. There is no love left. The throbbing of her hand seems to rhyme with the nightly hammering and sawing in the shed, fuelling her hatred. It is a hatred that underwrites the whole speech. The fact that a woman of strong religious conviction wants her husband dead says it all. For women in Lynette's social and economic circumstances, there seems no other way out.

Lynette Royce has now moved into the back bedroom, thank God. It's been a bit of a time, these last few weeks. I got a knife on the bedroom door lock and managed to get the paint off so it works, I can lock it at night now. Makes it a bit safer. I just don't know what he might do next, after the things he's said to me. Coming in, throwing things. Spoiling things in the house. What's the point of trying to keep things nice? I keep my room clean, I make my own meals when he's out. It's like a pigsty down there.

I tried to clean it up after he'd pulled everything out of the kitchen cupboard and smashed it, but I cut my hand quite bad on a bit of glass from the sauce bottle, I think it was, and I had to leave it. I should have had stitches really. It's funny, I thought it was tomato ketchup.

'Serves you fucking right,' he says. 'Cleaning up. You're always cleaning up. Leave it. Fucking LEAVE IT!' and something's exploded in my head and he must have hit my ear. My hand's full of blood but it's my ear that hurts. 'Don't you swear in this house! You stop saying your foul language to me, I won't have it. Don't swear!' and I'm hanging on to the edge of the sink to stop from falling over, I'm going dizzy. It makes me ill to hear bad words said before God and he knows it and he says it all the more, over and over, and my hand's under the tap and my head's swimming and ringing loud and the water turns red.

That night, I mend the door lock with one hand, while my other hand is throbbing through the cloth, and I hear him hammering and sawing in the shed in the yard, like it's been for days now into the night, but I don't care any more about what he's doing, I don't care, and I don't care if God doesn't want me to say it, I wish he were dead. I wish he were dead.

Serious Money *by Caryl Churchill*

This is a cutting satire on the 'Greed is good' society of the 1980s. It is written in verse. Scilla Todd is a dealer on the London Stock Exchange. She is 'top drawer'. Landed gentry. Posh finishing school. Daddy is a stockbroker. A child of the 'hunting, shooting and fishing' fraternity with a cut-glass accent to match. She is in her twenties, attractive, intelligent, arrogant, ambitious, greedy and completely amoral. A dangerous enemy. You could cut your fingers on her competitive edge. She describes herself as having 'the cunning and connections of the middle class' and being 'as tough as a yob'. A good description – add the power and influence of the upper classes, and you've got her.

When her whizz-kid brother Jake, a paper dealer, is found shot after some lucrative dodgy dealing and a visit from the DTI, she turns detective to find out who murdered him. From the first line of this speech it's easy to work out her priorities. It won't be a surprise to find she is more interested in getting her share of Jake's millions than finding out who killed him. Nothing personal. Nobody leaves Scilla out of a deal.

Don't get hung up on the rhyming couplets. The dialogue must sound completely naturalistic. Communicate her relish, make her explanations clear. You can almost smell the adrenalin rush as she describes the cut and thrust of trading. It's the buzz of gambling for high stakes. She loves what she does. It's a bigger 'buzz' than anything she's ever experienced. She lives 'on a high' and will be burnt-out by the time she's thirty-five. In the meantime, she's a tough corporate cookie who intends to keep her end up in a man's world. After the City she will be Wall Street's next rising star. And can't you just tell.

Scilla He was making serious money.

So Zac went back to Corman and I thought I'd better go to work despite Jake being dead because Chicago comes in at one twenty and I hate to miss it. I work on the floor of Liffe, the London International Financial Futures Exchange.

Trading options and futures looks tricky if you don't understand it.
But if you're good at market timing you can make out like a bandit.
  (It's the most fun I've had since playing cops and robbers with
  Jake when we were children.)
A simple way of looking at futures is take a commodity,
  coffee, cocoa, sugar, zinc, pork bellies, copper, aluminium, oil –
  I always think pork bellies is an oddity.
  (They could just as well have a future in chicken wings.)
Suppose you're a coffee trader and there's a drought in Brazil like
  last year or suppose there's a good harvest, either way you might
  lose out,
So you can buy a futures contract that works in the opposite
  direction so you're covered against loss, and that's what futures
  are basically about.
But of course you don't have to take delivery of anything at all.
You can buy and sell futures contracts without any danger of
  ending up with ten tons of pork bellies in the hall.
On the floor of Liffe the commodity is money.
You can buy and sell money, you can buy and sell absence of
  money, debt, which used to strike me as funny.

For some it's hedging, for most it's speculation.
In New York they've just introduced a futures contract in inflation.
  (Pity it's not Bolivian inflation, which hit forty thousand per cent.)
I was terrified when I started because there aren't any girls and
  they line up to watch you walk,
And every time I opened my mouth I felt self-conscious because of
  the way I talk.

I found O levels weren't much use, the best qualified people are
  street traders.
But I love it because it's like playing a cross between roulette and
  space invaders.

Speed-the-Plow *by David Mamet*

This is a satire set in the sycophantic world of Hollywood.

Karen is a young woman in her twenties with ambitions to work in the film industry. She is gorgeous (Madonna played the part in the original production), idealistic, but perhaps not as naïve as she seems. She is a 'temp' in the offices of Bobby Gould, newly promoted head of production for a big studio. Gould, twice her age and an 'industry whore', is 'on a bet' with a friend that he can't get Karen into bed.

It is late at night. Karen has come round to Gould's apartment to give a report on an 'arty' book he has asked her to read for him. He says he wants her opinion. He thinks it's a load of pretentious twaddle. It hasn't a cat-in-hell's chance of being made into a movie. He has used it as 'bait' to get Karen to come round.

But to Karen, reading the book has been a life-changing experience which resonates powerfully with her own situation. She identifies totally with the Tramp's quest for truth and meaning and is almost inarticulate in her efforts to convey the book's visionary impact to Bobby – the powerful effect it has had on her. She alternates between reading from the book, filling in the background and offering her own explanation of what it means. She reads with messianic fervour, colouring the words, giving every sentence maximum effect. She must make him understand. They have had a few drinks, which has heightened her zeal. The lights are low, the atmosphere, intimate.

What is Karen's agenda? She has no illusions about why Gould has invited her. Yet she came. Is she an innocent abroad, bringing her passion and idealism to bear on a cynical Tinseltown reaching out to the better man in Gould? Or is she just like everyone else? On the make? Using Gould? Trading on her beauty and sexual power to advance her career? David Mamet never spells it out. It's for you to decide.

Karen He puts his hand on the child's chest, and he says 'heal,' as if he felt he had the power to heal him, he calls on God . . . it's in here . . . something to the effect that if *ever* in his life he had the power, any power, that now is the time . . . list . . . (*She reads.*) '. . . in that lonely place, the low place, the tramp, under the bridge, he finds him. Faced with his troubles, and pours out his heart.' We hear the rain, and we see, in his misery, it is forgotten, wet, cold . . . and the problems which assaulted him: *they do not disappear*, but they are forgotten. He says: years later: it did not occur to him 'til then that this was happiness. That the thing which he lacked, he says, was *courage*. What does the Tramp say? 'All fears are one fear. Just the fear of death. And we accept it, then we are at peace.' And so, you see, and so all of the *events* . . . the *stone*, the *instrument*, the *child* which he met, *led* him there . . . in his . . . yes, you see – I know that you see – and that's, that's to me, that's the perfection of the story, when I *read* it . . . I almost, I wanted to sit, I saw, I almost couldn't come to you, the *weight* of it . . . (*Pause.*) You know what I mean. He says that the radiation . . . *all* of it, the planes, the televisions, clocks, all of it *is to the one end*. To *change* us – to, to *bring about a change* – all radiation has been sent by God. To change us. Constantly. To this new thing. And that we needn't feel frightened. That it comes from God. And I felt empowered. (*Pause.*) Empowered.

4.48 Psychosis *by Sarah Kane*

This is an uncompromising piece of theatre about depressive illness and suicide. Tragically it was Sarah Kane's last play.

The piece is about a woman for whom the pain of living is so acute, no other option but ending it makes sense. Look at the language in this section – how the writer uses words like 'cadaver', 'buried', 'decaying', 'grave', 'gallows' – all grimly pre-emptive of the character's fate and reflective of her state of mind. Its register shifts between long seamless sentences, emphatic repetitions, paranoid observations, angry outbursts and fragments of anguished poetry. It's as if we are privy to an unedited stream of consciousness.

Most of us experience depression at some time or another. Times when misery disables us and self-esteem is rock bottom. We are trapped in a cycle of fear and self-loathing – no tears, no hope, no point. Use it. This is the place from which this play is written. How has the character arrived here? The play offers no substantive history. The character's age is flexible. But she is not old. You must create your own 'back story'. What matters above everything else is that you grasp the nettle of her pain with the same gut-wrenching honesty the writer has dared to engage with. No mean task.

It wasn't for long, I wasn't there long. But drinking bitter black coffee I catch that medicinal smell in a cloud of ancient tobacco and something touches me in that still sobbing place and a wound from two years ago opens like a cadaver and a long buried shame roars its foul decaying grief.

A room of expressionless faces staring blankly at my pain, so devoid of meaning there must be evil intent.

Dr This and Dr That and Dr Whatsit who's just passing and thought he'd pop in to take the piss as well. Burning in a hot tunnel of dismay, my humiliation complete as I shake without reason and stumble over words and have nothing to say about my 'illness' which anyway amounts only to knowing that there's no point in anything because I'm going to die. And I am deadlocked by that smooth psychiatric voice of reason which tells me there is an objective reality in which my body and mind are one. But I am not here and never have been. Dr This writes it down and Dr That attempts a sympathetic murmur. Watching me, judging me, smelling the crippling failure oozing from my skin, my desperation clawing and all-consuming panic drenching me as I gape in horror at the world and wonder why everyone is smiling and looking at me with secret knowledge of my aching shame.

Shame shame shame.
Drown in your fucking shame.

Inscrutable doctors, sensible doctors, way-out doctors, doctors you'd think were fucking patients if you weren't shown proof otherwise, ask the same questions, put words in my mouth, offer chemical cures for congenital anguish and cover each other's arses until I want to scream for you, the only doctor who ever touched me voluntarily, who looked me in the eye, who laughed at my gallows humour spoken in the voice from the newly-dug grave, who took the piss when I shaved my head, who lied and said it was nice to see me. Who lied. And said it was nice to see me. I trusted you, I loved you, and it's not losing you that hurts me, but your bare-faced fucking falsehoods that masquerade as medical notes.

Your truth, your lies, not mine.

And while I was believing that you were different and that you maybe even felt the distress that sometimes flickered across your face and threatened to erupt, you were covering your arse too. Like every other stupid mortal cunt.

To my mind that's betrayal. And my mind is the subject of these bewildered fragments.

Nothing can extinguish my anger.

And nothing can restore my faith.

This is not a world in which I wish to live.

The Censor *by Anthony Neilson*

Fontaine is a young actress whose film has been banned by the British Censor on the grounds of its explicit sexual content. She has come to his office to dispute the ruling and make a case for her film.

She is intelligent, sexy, uninhibited, honest, challenging and intuitive. She uses sex to get what she wants and appeals to the Censor by removing her blouse, fondling his genitals and offering herself to him. She wants him to understand that her film has an emotional agenda behind the hard core imagery. Characters. Subtext. Detail. Her sexual candour gets under his skin and during the course of several unconsummated encounters she inveigles information out of him about his private life – his rocky marriage, his wife's infidelity and his sexual incapacity.

At this point in the play she is speculating about the reasons for the Censor's impotence. Why else wouldn't he respond to her? Is there some explanation buried in his past? She begins to create a scenario pieced from information she has gleaned from previous meetings. Like a detective she sets out her theories, getting closer and closer to the mark. She watches like a hawk, reading his reaction to each suggestion, titillating him with the truth about himself. She speculates. She probes. She picks over the possible reasons for his impotence until she hits on something close. His reaction to the word 'taboo' gives her the final clue to his coprophilia and the sexual fantasy that has shamed him into impotence. Her hand is on his crotch and she feels him respond. She understands. She accepts. It is her acceptance of his 'deviance' that finally arouses him and enables him to perform.

She has proven her point that there is more to the sexual act and more to her film than he has given her credit for.

Fontaine I was right about one of your parents being ill, wasn't I? There were many infidelities because of that illness. You saw how sex can destroy lives. But they loved each other too, and that was the most confusing thing. Because for all your talk about sex meaning love, it's *you* that can't bring them together. If you could, you wouldn't still be with your wife. No, sex is as much a mystery to you as happiness is. Something you can only watch and envy. But all that's obvious. There's something more specific.

Your impotence isn't medical. This is about shame.

You have a fantasy you're ashamed of.

You think of your wife as this deeply sexual being but you know even she wouldn't approve of it. Maybe you even asked her to do it once.

Yes and she was disgusted, wasn't she? And if this highly sexual woman could be so disgusted, who else would ever be different?

But you know there are girls that do it. You've seen it on the screen. Girls are being forced to degrade themselves to feed the sordid fantasies of misfits like you. And you hate those misfits, don't you? You hate them because they're too weak to rise above their desires. And where are we if we can't rise above our desires? You've done it. But you've paid a price, haven't you?

So what could this fantasy be?

If it was sado-masochistic you could easily indulge it with prostitutes, and anyway you're visual not tactile. This is about watching. Watching something taboo. Somewhere in your childhood, you saw this thing and had your first strong sexual feeling. You haven't buried it. You know what it is because you think about it when you masturbate.

Pause.

What did you see? Was it inside?

Pause. Her hand on his crotch.

No. Outside then? (*Pause.*) Something taboo.
Something violent? (*Pause.*) No.

Pause. She smiles.

Oh, Mr Censor. How beautiful. How absolutely beautiful.

Knives in Hens *by David Harrower*

The play is set in a pre-industrial community where flour is milled by stone, horses pull ploughs and village life is narrow, God-fearing and internecine. Young Woman is the wife of ploughman 'Pony' William. She leads a limited and dutiful life helping him farm his land. She is illiterate and struggles with a childlike vocabulary to interpret the inscrutability of her world.

In scenes before this pivotal speech, Young Woman hears husband William in the barn with another woman and flies across the village to the house of the miller, Gilbert Horn. Gilbert is hated and feared but he has a kind of mystery about him. He writes, reads books and has aspirations beyond village life. Young Woman is fascinated but repelled by him. She accuses Gilbert of bewitching her husband. Furious, Gilbert tells her in no uncertain terms what her husband is up to.

Traumatised by events and incomprehensible feelings for Gilbert, Young Woman stands for hours outside his house until finally he wraps her in a blanket and brings her back into the warm. In a trance-like state she sits at the table and writes. When she wakes, sheets of paper are covered in writing. Has Gilbert bewitched her too? When he tells her she held the pen herself, it is beyond comprehension.

In this speech, Young Woman reads aloud what she has written. We are witnessing a kind of miracle – like the naming of things in the Book of Genesis. She reads slowly, like someone discovering something precious. The language is poetic, almost translucent as faith; self-discovery and understanding open like a flower before her. It articulates emotions about a natural world that is more than the sum of all its parts. What she finds on the page puts her in touch with the beauty, pain, mystery and transience of the scheme of things and her place in it.

What are these new feelings she has for Gilbert, about the village and her faithless husband? The more she understands, the closer she gets to God.

When Gilbert leaves the village, it will need a new miller.

Young Woman (*looks at the pen, sees the paper, reads*) 'This is me. I live now. Others have, more will. I was born here because God wanted it. He had me sit in my mother till I could look at all that is His world. Every thing I see and know is put in my head by God. Every thing He created is there every day, sunrise to sundown, earth to sky. It cannot be touched or held the way I touch a table or hold the reins of a horse. It cannot be sold or cooked. His world is there, in front of my eyes. All I must do is push names into what is there the same as when I push my knife into the stomach of a hen. This is how I know God is there. I look at a tree and say tree then walk on. The tree is God. It is always God. But there is more. I know there is more of the tree that is God which I have no names for. Every name I have will take me closer to Him. This is how I will know God better. A puddle I can see under. A tree when it is blown by the wind. A carrot that is sweeter than the others. The cold earth under a rock. The warm breath of a tired horse. A man's face in the evening after work. The sound a woman makes when no one hears her. Only when I am deserving will I learn the names. This is what the village has always said. I know now I must find out the names for myself. If I stand and look close at every thing God will reward me. This is how I will know God better. The village has lied. William has lied. It is not because I am young and they are old. God has given them nothing. I know this now. I see William ploughing a field. I do not have a name for the thing which is in my head. It is not envy. It is more than envy. It does not scare me. I must look close enough to discover what it is. Every thing in my head is put there by God. Every name I have will take me closer to Him.' This was me.

She picks up the pen and begins writing again.

'S not envy. No. What is it? What is it? What's this thing? (*Finishes writing.*) William. Tell me's not you done this. I've no torment or misery. Then it is God. It is God.

Cleo, Camping, Emmanuelle and Dick
by Terry Johnson

In this comedy by Terry Johnson the Carry On team – Sid James, Kenneth Williams and Barbara Windsor – are shooting *Carry on Cleo*.

The scene is Sid James's leaky caravan on set.

Imogen, a sexy young actress, has been working on the film. She is empty-headed, upperclass and self-obsessed. She probably only got into drama school because 'Daddy' was 'on the Board' and only works as an actress because of the size of her breasts. She has just had sex with Sid James, who is old enough to be her father. She is drunk, naked or semi-naked and looking for her clothes, which are scattered round the caravan. Having had his wicked way with her, Sid is keen to eject her before somebody comes, giving her search a comic urgency. Imogen wants to be noticed and taken seriously but is not above posing for a naked centre-fold or sleeping with a star to get on in the business. Drink has loosened her tongue. The speech is a wittering diatribe revealing how rootless and lonely she really is. She uses sex as a currency to get what she wants, but is neither sufficiently observant nor self-aware to realise that it buys her nothing more than disrespect and reinforcement of the image she seeks to jettison. The more she tells him how good other people think she is, the more she reveals her lack of self-esteem and the emptiness of the world she inhabits. She blames her physical attributes and other people's perceptions for blighting her career but anyone who thinks Ibsen's women don't have breasts doesn't have much of a head start in their chosen career.

Her damaged behaviour makes her her own worst enemy.

Imogen I'm surprised you even remembered me. I'm flattered. I mean, who was I then? I was out and about, I know, but I'd barely left LAMDA and honestly I knew nothing. I *was* nothing. This is such a strange business. You get a job, you meet someone, you like them, you maybe sleep with them, the job ends, then you never see them again even though you always say you will. I made some really good friends on *When Dinosaurs Ruled the Earth*, except Raquel of course, but she doesn't make friends, she just takes the odd hostage. Thing is I haven't seen anyone since. Except there was a particularly persistent caveman who I did see once but his wife was pregnant and he just cried all evening. Everything's so . . . temporary. That's what's nice about working with you lot; you're one big happy family. I'd love to work with you lot again. You know what I wish? I wish I had smaller breasts. Then I'd get to play some women with small breasts, and they're always the best parts. I'd really like to play women with no breasts at all, you know, like in Ibsen. I should never have done the centrefold. I'm actually very versatile. 'An impressive multifaceted performance'; that's what they said about me as Jenny Grubb in *Loving*. And that wasn't just taking off the glasses and letting my hair down, that was *acting* actually. I was *acting* her repressed sexuality. What I'm saying is, I'm not just some stupid girl from Elmhurst with a fucked knee, you know. I'm not just the Countess of Cleavage; all right? It's so hard to convince people I'm a serious actress, but I really think it's beginning to happen. I've got an audition for the Royal Shakespeare Company? And last month I did *The Persuaders*. Only the pilot but both Roger Moore *and* Tony Curtis were very complimentary and said there was a very good chance my character could become a regular.

Top Girls *by Caryl Churchill*

This is a play solely about women. It is set in the early eighties during 'top girl' Mrs Thatcher's first term of office as Prime Minister. It addresses a tapestry of themes around the roles, expectations and shared experiences of women in Thatcher's 'there's no such thing as society', 'get rich quick' Britain.

Shona is a naïve, chirpy, brazen young woman of twenty-one who pretends to be several years older, and far more sophisticated that she actually is. She could have any accent.

Ambitious and career-orientated Nell in the Top Girls Employment Agency is interviewing her for a sales position. This is the only scene in the play in which Shona appears.

At first the interview seems to be going well. Shona impresses with her brash, self-interested, go-getting energy. Her enthusiasm for the high-flying end of the market – computers, video systems, etc. – is guaranteed to impress the energetic Nell. It is not until Nell asks her to expand a little on her present job that Shona's pitch falls apart. Her fantasy version of executive life on an expense account is laughably transparent. It is culled from a half-digested understanding of consumer manuals and advertising cliché. Her repetitions, back-trackings and improvised verbal constructions quickly reveal Shona as 'wet behind the ears', inventing and embellishing this ludicrous account of her day 'on the hoof'. By the end of the speech it's obvious she is a complete fraud.

Yet when her integrity is challenged, Shona is unabashed and blissfully unaware of how socially and educationally ill-equipped she is to be a beneficiary of the materialist culture she so obviously craves.

Shona My present job at present. I have a car. I have a Porsche. I go up the M1 a lot. Burn up the M1 a lot. Straight up the M1 in the fast lane to where the clients are, Staffordshire, Yorkshire, I do a lot in Yorkshire. I'm selling electric things. Like dishwashers, washing machines, stainless-steel tubs are a feature and the reliability of the programme. After-sales service, we offer a very good after-sales service, spare parts, plenty of spare parts. And fridges, I sell a lot of fridges, specially in the summer. People want to buy fridges in the summer because of the heat melting the butter and you get fed up standing the milk in a basin of cold water with a cloth over, stands to reason people don't want to do that in this day and age. So I sell a lot of them. Big ones with big freezers. Big freezers. And I stay in hotels at night when I'm away from home. On my expense account. I stay in various hotels. They know me, the ones I go to. I check in, have a bath, have a shower. Then I go down to the bar, have a gin and tonic, have a chat. Then I go into the dining room and have dinner. I usually have fillet steak and mushrooms, I like mushrooms. I like smoked salmon very much. I like having a salad on the side. Green salad. I don't like tomatoes.

Shakers Restirred *by John Godber*

Shakers is the name of a cocktail bar in a northern town – although it could be anywhere. It's where Mr and Mrs Trendy and Very Trendy rub shoulders with 'chinless yuppies', blokes on the make and on the beer, and designer-clad check-out girls pose, knock back exotic cocktails and 'eye up' the merchandise. It's a plastic world of superficial glamour and empty values.

The play is set in the mid-eighties. Nicky is one of four exploited and disenchanted waitresses who work at Shakers. Each has a story to tell and at some point in the play, each steps out of the main action to share it with us. Rich audition pickings for you and well worth looking for if this one doesn't suit.

Nicky is in her late teens, early twenties. She is attractive, working class and none too bright. Like the others she hates her job. And she's been offered an escape route. It's a job as a dancer on a cruise ship. She has been boasting about it to the other girls, but hasn't been entirely frank. Once she's on her own it's a different story. She couldn't tell them but she's confiding in us.

She's in a real state about the prospect of leaving family and friends, not to mention the prospect of dancing topless. As she says, her 'mind's gone haywire'. She's not entirely certain what's in store. The job has been sold to her by a lecherous employer, as 'tasteful', 'classy', 'all in the interests of art', but it's clear she'll be nothing more than a bit of scantily-clad titillation for the punters. Not much different from her present job. But Nicky needs so much to see this as a big opportunity. This is her exit route from the joyless grind.

But look how often 'I'm sure . . .' pops up in the second half of the monologue as Nicky struggles to rationalise her fears as the understandable nerves of someone on the threshold of a Big Adventure. Her final questions are full of pathos. What has a girl like Nicky got to look forward to?

The lights fade. A spotlight outlines **Nicky**. *The others freeze.*

Nicky I know they're jealous of me. I don't blame them, no one wants to stay here. It's funny though, now I can escape, I'm bloody scared to death. Nine months, it's a long time, what if I don't make any friends? What if I get seasick, or food poisoning, or get lost somewhere in a forest and have to live with a tribe of Eskimos and never come home again? I know I'm being stupid. My mind's gone haywire. But deep down I'm a panicker, I can't help it, but I am. And I know it's what I want, but in reality it's frightening leaving it all . . . your mum, your dad, your mates. I'm excited as well though, don't get me wrong. I wouldn't forgo the opportunity, it's a chance in a lifetime: travel, freedom, celebrity. Oh yeah, I've definitely got to go! But the actual job? I wouldn't tell the others but more than anything I'm apprehensive about that. I've got to lose some weight for a start, some of the costumes are ever so small, sequins and all that stuff, but there is some topless as well. It's classy, it's all part of the dancing. But it's getting over that first time, isn't it? Then I'm sure I'll be all right. You see, to be honest it took me about four days to get them out when we went to Ibiza and then I laid on my front. I suppose though they're all right, even though I'm not Bridget Neilson. And they did look at them so if they were awful they wouldn't have had me. Like I said, I'm sure I'll get used to it. It's all the excitement, it makes you nervous. I don't know black from white. But I'm sure it will be brilliant, I'm sure it will. I mean, the world will be my oyster, I can't believe it! That's the thing though, isn't it? What do you do when a dream comes true? What do you dream of then?

Spoonface Steinberg *by Lee Hall*

This is a wise and profound one-person play about love and dying. It is lyrical, funny and immensely moving. There are any number of audition pieces to choose from.

An actor of either sex can play *Spoonface Steinberg*, although grown-up women have hitherto played it. The task is to get into the heart and mind of a gifted autistic child.

Spoonface is the child of Jewish academics; a genius with anything to do with numbers, but unable to engage emotionally with people and unaffected by events.

This section describes Spoonface's journey from feeling poorly to a diagnosis of terminal cancer. See how linear the language is. One thought runs chronologically into the next without any significant punctuation. It's as if she can't keep more than one thought in her head at once. There is no pause to assess the impact her story is having on her audience, no sense of its import. Nor does she seem able to allocate any emotional weight to even the direst of events. For instance, there is no difference between having a drink of pop or getting cancer. The tone is factual and detached. You must disengage from the drama of the situation for its full impact to be felt.

Spoonface has no complex agenda. Hers is to 'see the world in a grain of sand' but make no judgement about what she sees. The actor should resist the obvious choice of 'playing a child', letting the simplicity of Spoonface's voice speak through them. There is not even a hint of self-pity. Research into autistic behaviour will help you take an objective view of Spoonface's disability. Avoid sentimentality – it is always a trap when playing a disabled character.

Spoonface Steinberg When I first started feeling funny, that is, when I still had hair – it was hardly noticeable at first – that was there was hardly nothing wrong except I was tired a bit – but then Mam was very worried that I was thinner and thinner and one day I might fade away to a speck – and that I was looking peaky – but because I'm backwards then I wasn't very good at saying what is wrong – so she took me straight to the doctor in case I disappeared – and the doctor looked at me like this . . . and he said – 'Oh deary me, Spoonface will have to go straight to the hospital' – which is where I went – it was all right as I had been once before to do the numbers – they were all very nice to me and the doctors held on to my hand and stuff and they all smiled which means something is wrong – and then Mam looked greyish and they said they were going to have to put me in a tube, which was quite horrible as I am only little – I did not wish to go into the tube but they said I would have to on account of being so thin – and inside the tube they would find out what it was – so I went in the tube and Mam was watching when I went in and waved bye bye – and then all these computers went off and stuff – and they did all this dialling and whirring and then there was some rays or something – and I was in there like it was a space machine but it never went anywhere except in the hospital even though it took ages – and I waited and all the computers were doing different numbers and all the information was going everywhere and that – and then it came time for me to come out and when I came out there was Mam and the doctor waiting and they said hello and I was allowed out – the doctor said he would have to check the switches and that we should all go into a room where Mam could cry and I could play with Lego – when I was in the room I got a drink of pop and Mam said it was unexpected that we would go straight to the hospital and go into a tube – then the doctor came back and said that he had got an answer off the machines and the answer was – that I was going to die.

Adult Child/Dead Child *by Claire Dowie*

The child in Claire Dowie's one-person play is written to be played by either sex. An adult who has to some extent 'come through' picks over the bones of an abusive childhood. It is a painful narrative, addressed directly to the audience, making it rich territory for audition pieces.

Let's call the unnamed character in the play Child, and let's make her female.

Child has suffered unimaginable abuse at the hands of her parents – tied to chairs, locked in cupboards. No understanding. No communication. Punishment. Lack of love is a big empty hole in Child's stomach. Hurt and ignored, lonely and unloved, Child invents an imaginary friend called Benji. Someone else to take the heat and the blame.

In the section I have chosen, Child describes Benji's bad behaviour, which is of course her own angry response to her treatment. Benji swears, steals, throws tantrums, smashes things. The more Benji misbehaves, the more Child is punished. The more Child is punished the angrier she gets and the more Benji misbehaves. How else can she express the pain she feels? This 'split self' is a necessary strategy for Child's survival.

Benji is named after a neighbour's much-loved dog, described affectionately by her as 'a monster and a horror and a terror' and herein lies the conundrum of Child's existence and the duality the actor must seek to express. For Benji is not just Child's only friend, but also the instrument of her rage. The actor must draw the audience to the very heart of an abused child's anguish.

_____

The only time our worlds collided was when Benji did something wrong and I got the blame for it.

At school I had to see a child psychologist. (What an idiot.)

Benji loved words like outlaw, hooligan, gangster, delinquent, vandal – she thought they sounded good, romantic, exciting.

Benji would swear. It wouldn't have been so bad if it was just swearing, if it was just swearing, if Benji just swore, it wouldn't have been so bad. But it wasn't, wasn't just swearing, Benji stole. She stole. She stole money, from my parents, from my school mates, from everybody, she needn't, she didn't have to, she didn't need it. And shoplifting, shoplifting and stealing things, silly things, she didn't need them, she stole a toy car once, she didn't need it, she didn't even like it, she threw it away later, and travelling, going off jaunting, playing truant from school, not turning up, just jaunting off anywhere, travelling around. And she shouted. And she shouted at people and threw things, she'd go mad and shout at people and throw things, tantrums, she had tantrums and shouted at people and threw things, threw things at the wall, all over the room, threw the furniture and the ornaments at the walls and all over the room and at people, she threw things at people and shouted at them and swore at them, she swore, it wouldn't have been so bad if she just swore but she didn't. She was wild, uncontrollable. She thought it was funny. I didn't. I never wanted to get into trouble, I never did want to get into all that trouble. They wouldn't believe me that it was Benji so I stopped telling them. It was just trouble all the time, trouble all the time and Benji was laughing. I couldn't control her. I couldn't stop her. She scared me.

The Gift *by Roy Williams*

Janet is a black woman in her twenties, born in England of
Jamaican parentage. A school dropout, and pregnant at
fifteen, Janet has always been the butt of her mother's
disapproval. We find her at the graveside of her brother,
Andy, a college boy – the apple of his mother's eye – who
had been stabbed in a knife fight. Everyone thinks it was an
unprovoked attack, but Janet, who witnessed the incident,
knows better.

Here she is addressing her dead brother directly. The
speech begins with shared memories of childhood; of
Auntie Bernice, a larger than life relative from Jamaica who
claims to have the gift of raising spirits from the dead.
Perhaps because she has invoked the memory of her psychic
auntie, Andy's presence begins to feel more real. Janet starts
to lose control. Andy was always the favourite. Andy had all
their mother's love. She was the one who always got it
wrong. Little does her mother know! Andy wasn't the goody
two-shoes everybody thought. Raw jealousy and a lifetime
of resentment bubble to the fore. She uses the language of a
kids' slanging match, familiar territory in this relationship.
See how it tips into her mother's Jamaican vernacular the
more she 'tells it how it is'. As she desecrates Andy's grave
he becomes a real and terrifying presence, back from the
dead to taunt and belittle her. By the end of the speech you
must make us feel he's really there.

Perhaps after all it is Janet, not Aunt Bernice, who has
'the gift'.

Janet (*laughing*) . . . then she lifted her up, right in the air – yu shoulda seen it, man, Mum's face. Strong, man. 'Member when she told us once, she could pick up a whole horse by herself? And yu believed her, yer soft git. And yu were afraid of her, cos she loved tellin' ghost stories, hidin' under my covers whenever we heard the footsteps. 'Auntie Bernice is comin' to get me!' That was yu. Scared little Andy, I remember that, yu fool. Yu know summin, it's weird, right, but I feel like . . . Andy, yu watchin' me? Andy? Shut the fuck up, Janet. Hear wat, Mum knows 'bout the caff so yu know wass gonna 'appen now? She gonna go on and on about it, yu know how she stay, me and Ryan should sell up, prove her right, Janet's fucked up again. Cos compared to yu, I'm nuttin, ennit, broth? I hate, fuckin' hate yu. I hate yu. I don't miss yu, wid yer snidy little bitchy comments, who yu tryin' to impress? Then yu actin' all hard, givin' it large, wat were yu thinkin', man? Wat was goin' thru yer head? Now yu tryin' to mek me feel bad, wat you want?

She starts jumping on the headstone, she kicks the flowers, picks up some pebbles and dirt and throws them at it.

(*In a rage.*) Wat . . .

She feels the wind again. She turns around suddenly. Someone is there with her, she can feel it. She can hear something.

(*Terrified.*) No.

Getting Out *by Marsha Norman*

There are two main characters in Marsha Norman's play. There is Arlene, a thin, drawn woman in her late twenties from downtown Kentucky who has been in and out of prison all her life, and Arlie her aggressive, hateful younger self. (Her accent, says the author, has a 'country' twang.)

Arlene is now out on parole after serving an eight-year sentence for robbery and second-degree murder. She has been housed by the authorities in a squalid one-roomed apartment; while she was 'inside' her outlook was changed by a prison chaplain who became her friend and mentor. He convinced her that God would find a means to take away the 'bad' Arlie so the 'good' Arlene could prevail. Now she is determined to be the good Arlene.

In this scene, upstairs neighbour Ruby, an older rehabilitating ex-con, interrupts an argument between Arlene and Carl (her former pimp). Carl has tracked Arlene down and is pressing her to go with him. Ruby 'sees Carl off' but for Arlene it is a sharp reminder of how close she is to Arlie and another way of life.

This Faustian battle between Arlie and Arlene is re-enacted in this speech. Arlene tells Ruby how she was abandoned by the prison chaplain who had been summarily transferred to another prison; how she completely 'lost it' and tried to kill her alter ego with a dinner fork.

This is a difficult speech with sudden emotional twists and shifts. At the beginning the language is raw and dislocated revealing a delusional and disordered mental state. Words stutter out of her, as distress mounts with the memory of events. Then the language 'uncreases' as her mental health begins to heal. But Arlene is always close to the emotional wire. Anger and grief are never far off and by the end of the speech she completely loses control, weeping and screaming into Ruby's lap. What is this awful grief about? A lost 'good' version of herself? Youth squandered? Opportunities gone?

This outburst is the beginning of the healing process for Arlene – of coming to terms with Arlie and reconciling herself with her past. Only then will she be able to move on.

Arlene They tol me . . . after I's out an it was all over . . . they said after the chaplain got transferred . . . I didn't know why he didn't come no more til after . . . they said it was three whole nights at first, me screamin to God to come git Arlie an kill her. They give me this medicine an though I's better . . . then that night it happened, the officer was in the dorm doin count . . . an they didn't hear nuthin but they come back out where I was an I'm standin there telling em to come see, real quiet I'm tellin em, but there's all this blood all over my shirt an I got this fork I'm holdin real tight in my hand . . . (*Clenches one hand now, the other hand fumbling with the buttons as if she's going to show* **Ruby**.) this fork, they said Doris stole it from the kitchen an give it to me so I'd kill myself and shut up botherin her . . . an there's all these holes all over me where I been stabbin myself an I'm saying Arlie is dead for what she done to me, Arlie is dead and it's God's will . . . I didn't scream it, I was jus sayin it over and over . . . Arlie is dead, Arlie is dead . . . they couldn't git that fork outta my hand til . . . I woke up in the infirmary an they said I almost died. They said they's glad I didn't. (*Smiling.*) They said did I feel better now an they was real nice, bringing me chocolate puddin . . . I'd be eatin or jus lookin at the ceiling an git a tear in my eye, but it'd jus dry up, you know, it didn't run out or nuthin. An then pretty soon, I's well, an officers was saying they's seein such a change in me an givin me yarn to knit sweaters an how'd I like to have a new skirt to wear an sometimes lettin me chew gum. They said things ain't never been as clean as when I's doin the housekeepin at the dorm. (*So proud.*) An then I got in the honor cottage an nobody was foolin with me no more or nuthin. An I didn't git mad like before or nuthin. I just done my work an knit . . . an I don't think about it, what happened, cept . . . (*Now losing control.*) people here keep callin me Arlie an . . . (*Has trouble saying 'Arlie'.*) I didn't mean to do it, what I done . . . I did . . . (*This is very difficult.*) I mean, Arlie was a pretty mean kid, but I did . . . (*Very quickly.*) I didn't know what I . . . (*Breaks down completely, screaming, crying, falling over into* **Ruby**'s *lap.*) Arlie! (*Grieving for this lost self.*)

Cigarettes and Chocolate
by Anthony Minghella

Gemma is an over-sensitive, politically and socially committed middle-class professional in her late twenties/ early thirties. One day, much to the dismay of family and friends she makes a conscious decision to stop speaking. She takes a holiday abroad, speaks lovingly to her friends, then on a day designated by a red cross on her calendar, she ceases to communicate. 'Like killing yourself' she says, and it has a similar impact. Friends try to make sense of her silence. All in different ways and for different reasons blame themselves.

But Gemma's reasons are far more complex than her friends can know. In this speech, which falls right at the end of the play, she explains them to the audience. How can a caring person effect change in a world of injustice and pain? The question is too difficult. The rush, the roar, the madness is too much for her. Her garrulous and self-interested friends who all want a piece of her, have each made a contribution to her trauma.

A photograph of a self-immolating Buddhist monk making a wordless protest against injustices in Tibet is a kind of talisman for Gemma. It has a potency that words do not. Silence is both 'direct action' and retreat.

Nothing has an impact unless it affects individuals personally she argues. How can she make people think? Care? Notice? She balances life's trivia (cigarettes, chocolate, the mindless repetition of consumer existence) against global injustice, poverty and homelessness. She wrestles with the insignificance of individual action, political correctness, argument, news, art; the meaninglessness and the senselessness of words in the face of human pain and repression. It is the small, secret, silent things that matter, she maintains. Although Gemma's silence has all the ingredients of obsession and control, there is a kind of wisdom in it too.

Play the silences as well as the words. They have their own impact and dramatic power.

Gemma When you stop speaking, it's like stopping eating. The first day there's something thrilling, and new, before the pain begins. The pain where you want to give up, where you can think of nothing else.

Then the second day, you feel wretched, the third delirious, and then suddenly there's no appetite, it shrinks, it shrinks, until the prospect of speaking, the thought of words retching from the mouth, how ugly and gross it seems.

Nothing changes.

How to stop people in their tracks, and make them think. Only if you're starving, if it's your son lying in your arms, or you think he might be in that discarded pile of mutilated bodies, or there's no milk in your breast and the baby's crying, or the radiation is leaking into your child's lungs, or the lead or the nitrates or the, or the, or the and all the while skirts get longer, skirts get shorter, skirts get longer, skirts get shorter, poetry is written, the news is read, I buy a different butter at the store and have my hair permed, straightened, coloured, cut, lengthened, all the while my hair keeps growing, I throw away all my skirts, a black bag to Oxfam, lately I've been at Oxfam buying back my skirts. I've stripped the pine and painted the pine, pulled out the fireplaces and put them back in, I'm on the pill, I'm off the pill, I'm on the pill, I'm off the pill. I'm listening to jazz, swing, jazz, swing, I'm getting my posters framed. I'm telling my women's group everything. I'm protesting. I'm protesting. I've covered my wall with postcards, with posters, with postcards, with posters. No this. Out them. In these. Yes those. No this. Out them. In these. Yes those. The rows. The rows with my friends, my lovers. What were they about? What did they change? The fact is, the facts are, nothing is changed. Nothing has been done. There is neither rhyme nor reason, just tears, tears, people's pain, people's rage, their aggression. And silence.

Look, already it's happening here, the weight of words, the torrent, all the words being said seep into each other, the rage, the protest all clotting together, sit and listen to the wireless and run the wheel of the tuner, spin the dial, hear them all at it, in all languages, pouring out. This is, after all, our first punishment – Babel – saying so much to say nothing. Doing so much to do nothing. Because the power to arrest, to stop us short in our tracks, what does that?

Pause.

But the silence, listen, how rich it is, how pregnant, how full . . .

Pause.

What do you remember? When all is said and done? A kiss? The taste of someone's lips? A view? A breath? A tune? The weight of your grandmother's coffin? The veins on your mother's legs. The white lines on her stomach.

Don't speak for a day and then start looking. The senses are sharp. Look at the world about its business. The snarl. The roar. Skin stretched over the teeth. The madness.

The law is frightened of silence. It has words for the defendant who becomes mute. The wrath of God. Mute by malice. But it's not silence which is the punishment. Words. WORDS are the punishment.

A silence.

beautiful
last year it was cigarettes,
the year before chocolate,
but this is the best.

The Aria. 'Mache dich, mein Hertze, rein' from Bach's St Matthew Passion. *Magnificent. Released.*

The Memory of Water *by Shelagh Stephenson*

Catherine, the black sheep of the family, returns from Spain to join her sisters for their mother's funeral. She is thirty-three, self-obsessed, irritating, addictive, unmarried (but desperately wanting to be), lonely and 'in therapy'. Sibling rivalries are rife; skeletons emerge from cupboards and old battles are re-rehearsed as the sisters allocate blame and unpick grievances in the claustrophobia of their mother's house.

Xavier, the latest in a long line of Catherine's men, has just finished their relationship in a perfunctory phone call from Spain. Xavier was expected at the funeral and until now Catherine pretended all was well with her relationship. She seems to be tough. But after a supportive word from a sister, her mother's death and Xavier's call, all her fragile coping mechanisms fall apart. Everything that is wrong with her life tumbles out in a scarcely punctuated stream of consciousness. She hardly draws breath. Nor should the actor. Earlier she seemed impervious to her mother's death – but how much of this sudden outpouring relates to Xavier's call and how much to the orphaned little girl in her jumping up and down? Think about how angry and abandoned we feel when someone dies; how much easier to focus on little things, when big things seem too difficult. The language is opaque, exposes raw pain, a complete lack of self-esteem and a frightening inability to cope. Under all the self-justification and blame we should sense the extent to which Catherine is a victim of her dysfunctional Catholic family and how far her self-obsessed nature makes her the inevitable architect of her own misery.

Catherine Yeah. Yeah. He said he'd ring back later.

She gets up.

So. What is there still to do? Shall we sort the drawers out? There's all the jewellery and stuff –

She goes to the dressing-table drawer and begins to rummage through it, taking things out haphazardly.

God, he's so funny sometimes, he's so apologetic. He was almost crying on the phone, you should have heard him. It's just a real drag he can't come, he's so lovely. Did I ever show you his photo? He's got beautiful teeth. I mean, he really, really wanted to come. It's just hopeless, you know, running a restaurant and everything, you never get any time off.

Fuck it!

Silence. She bursts into racking sobs.

I went to this counsellor – did I tell you this? – or a therapist or something and she said I had this problem and the problem was, I give too much, I just do too much for other people, I'm just a very giving person, and I never get any credit for any of it. I haven't even got any friends. I mean, I have but I don't like most of them, especially the women, and I try really hard, it's just I'm very sensitive and I get taken for a ride, nothing ever goes right, every time, I mean, every time it's the same – like with men. What is it with men? I mean, I don't have a problem with men or anything. I love men. I've been to bed with seventy-eight of them, I counted, so obviously there's not a problem or anything, it's just he didn't even apologise or anything and how can he say on the phone he doesn't want to see me any more? I mean, why now? Why couldn't he have waited? I don't know what to do, why does it always go wrong? I don't want to be on my own, I'm sick of people saying I'll be better off on my own, I'm not that sort of person, I can't do it. I did everything for him, I was patient and all the things you're supposed to be and people kept saying don't accept this from him, don't accept that, like, you know, when he stayed out all night, not very often, I mean once or twice, and everyone said tell him to fuck off, but how could I because what if he did? Because they all do, everyone I've ever met does, they all disappear and I don't know if it's me or what. I don't want to be on my own, I can't stand it, I know it's supposed to be great but I don't think it is. I can't help it, it's no good pretending, it's fucking lonely and I can't bear it.

Ten Tiny Fingers, Nine Tiny Toes
by Sue Townsend

This is a tragi-comedy written in 1989 but set in the futuristic world of 2001. A totalitarian government is in power. Society is divided into five classes. Only the upper echelons – Class 3 humans and above – are allowed to breed. Babies can be bought and sold. Babies born to the lower orders are illegal. The State's aim is that everyone should eventually be beautiful, healthy, intelligent and hard-working. Any child born with an imperfection is eliminated. Humans are allowed to live until the age of seventy then, having outlived their usefulness, are eliminated too.

Orderly is a 'patriot' in her thirties. A perfect depersonalised cog in the wheel of the State. She works in the Buxton Maternity Unit. She is efficient, practical and hard-working – well suited to her job title. She plays everything by the book. But cracks are beginning to appear in her orderly world. In this speech she shares some personal anxieties with the audience as she sets up a Conception Ceremony for an infertile Class 3 couple. She is 'a bag of nerves'. Her mum is refusing to do the patriotic thing and turn up for her lethal injection on her appointed Death Day. Orderly is less concerned about her mother than the impact her renegade behaviour will have on her. We can only guess what sanctions the State might take. She has used all her powers of persuasion, but to no avail.

A seam of anxiety runs through the speech as Orderly serves up her absurd brand of logic as common sense. It is implicit that the audience shares her perspective. 'Why can't my mother see it our way?' she is saying, in the topsy-turvy nightmare of her world.

By the end of the speech, the room is ready for the ceremony and Orderly slips briefly into her professional persona. But as she nervously picks her teeth with the card we see what a big worry it all is.

———————————

Orderly I keep thinking it's Friday. I'm off this weekend, going to see my mum, she's only got five months to go. Three days, five months. She's being difficult though, she says they'll have to come and get her, she won't do it herself. I'm hoping she'll change her mind, it could reflect badly on me. She doesn't see why she should have to go at all. She says she's fit and well and good for another twenty years. She thinks she's invincible. The invincible woman. I've said to her, 'What's the point of living on after seventy years? You're not working, you're not generating wealth, your brain will go, your body will fall apart. It's unpatriotic. You'll be a parasite.' She's still living in the old days when people died all over the place – on holiday, in the car, in shops. It was inconvenient and it caused a lot of disruption. People having days off work for funerals and rushing about with death certificates. I said, 'Mum, you're being selfish – it's a tiny injection and then a long sleep. You deserve it, you've worked hard' – but she wouldn't listen. I hope she'll be in, she sometimes goes off at the weekends – painting with an easel she found on a rubbish tip. She walks miles with this easel thing under her arm. She's a terrible embarrassment to me. And you know what she paints? The countryside! (*She laughs.*) Don't ask me why. She's got all these little *pictures* up on the walls in her room. It's a sign of senility. I mean, there are professionals whose job it is to paint pictures. *She* doesn't need to do it. I'm surprised she's got away with it for so long. And now this stubborn attitude she's taking towards Death Day. (*Determined.*) Well, she'll have to go along with it. I've booked a day off for it and I can't go chopping and changing – it's on the computer now, so that's final. It'll be a relief for me when she's gone. I can concentrate on my work. At the moment I'm a bag of nerves, wondering what the daft old bat will do next. If it gets out about the pictures . . .

She takes a card out of her pocket and checks the room.

Lucinda Darling. Husband Ralph. Government Section Three. Secular, religious and video ceremony. (*She shouts.*) Ready! Wheel 'em in. Ten seconds!

She stands and picks her teeth with the edge of the card.

I hope she'll be in.

Goliath *by Bryony Lavery*

This play is based on a book by Beatrix Campbell of the same name. It explores issues around community relations, the maintenance of law and order and final 'social meltdown' on three rough estates.

Originally a woman played all the characters.

This section is entitled 'Wor Latest Game'. ('Wor' is colloquial Geordie. You'll need to do some research to find out how it's used along with finding the meaning of other words like 'gan' and 'tabs'.) The scene is the Meadowell Estate on Tyneside.

Maureen is a Geordie in her late thirties, mother of Gary, a seventeen-year-old joyrider who has been killed in a spectacular police car chase, which is dramatised in Act One. He has become something of a cause célèbre on the estate. Pregnant and married at sixteen, Maureen is the product of a disadvantaged and marginalised underclass. She's uneducated and inadequate but she does her best. Now her only child is dead. The writer describes her as 'thin, vibrating with anxiety and depression. Woman of wood . . . stuck, harmless, kind, slow.' Short sentences, with line endings serving as punctuation, are sometimes left hanging in the air as Maureen's thoughts catch on moments of reverie or current grief.

While sorting through Gary's effects she finds a 'designer' teapot he gave her for a wedding anniversary present – a thoughtful gift, but stolen nevertheless. This and the ghetto blaster she finds hidden in his room trigger painful memories of Gary's lawless childhood and her lack of influence over his behaviour.

The speech should be played as if Maureen is not only picking through Gary's effects but also through seminal events that presaged the senseless end of his short rebellious existence. She's trying to make sense of it all.

To everyone else, Gary was a 'bad boy', but to Maureen he is her child, and for better or worse, she loved him.

Maureen *sorting, finds an eternal-bow teapot.*

He give us this teapot.
Happy Wedding Anniversary, he says.
Ah said 'Where's this from like?'
He says 'A shop.'

it's Eternal Bow
it's what ah've got everything in
but . . .

Discovers a ghetto blaster.

And *this* ghetto blaster was on top of his
wardrobe underneath a jacket!
Now why's *that* d'you think?

ten he was . . .
this started . . .
one night he's in and oot tha kitchen
he opens ma purse
takes some money oot
says he wants to go oot for fish and chips
I say it's too late
his dad says nowt

he pesters and pesters
I gan
'Okay, but be back by ten'
and he was.
I said 'Good boy.'

He's standing behind ma chair
Ah'm feeling funny
Ah say to my husband

'What's he daeing, like?'
His dad laughs and says 'He's
pretending he's got a knife
and he's stabbing you in the neck.'

I've found cider bottles under his bed
Ah think he had a drinking problem
on top of everything else!

he'd started being violent at home.

He hit wor.

eleven
he wouldn't go to school
He was *my* problem
I took him to school
the head says 'Oh, you're stopping?'
my lad says 'No.'
So the head says 'There's the door. Ooot.'
Ah've tried.
Bloody school didn't.
Ah've learned him the most I could
how to read
how to write
how to tell the time . . .

hit wor and said I wor a grass.

I knew I was losing him to the streets

last year
I discovered Gary in the *act* of breaking
into wor own newsagent's . . .
where wor gets wor tabs from!
I called the police from the call box.
They said 'You're grassing your own son?'
I said 'Yes.'

They said 'We've picked up your son.
Are you coming to get him?'
I said 'No. This is the only way I
can think of to get help!'

It's done no good.
He was in and out of prison all the time.

I did love him.

Sweet Panic *by Stephen Poliakoff*

Clare is a confident, elegant woman in her late thirties. She is a child psychologist, the product of late sixties and seventies liberalism. Originally from 'up north', her accent betrays small traces of her origins. She practises in central London. On the whole she is cool and professional, if a little controlling. But when she is attacked by an older client and stalked by the middle-class mother of another, her approach to her work and her ability to find solutions is severely challenged.

Throughout the play Clare gives us insights into the minds of her clients by slipping into loose characterisations of them. At the beginning of Act Two Clare tells us about Jess, a creative and confrontational thirteen-year-old from north London. Jess scarcely attends school. Instead she roams the streets and makes intricate models of things she sees and delivers them to Clare.

This speech (there are others of a similar ilk you might look at as well) is delivered 'into the eye' of the audience, as if the fourth wall has been temporarily removed. The acting challenge is to sustain Clare's character while at the same time see her creating the essence of Jess. It is important not to attempt a direct impersonation. Clare sees her job as entering the imaginations of her clients in order to see the world through their eyes – so in a way you're being asked to play two people at once. This theatrical device enables us to enter Jess's world with her and at the same time see her from Clare's perspective. Sometimes Jess's remarks about Clare's life are rather too close to the bone for comfort.

The models in Madame Tussaud's represent the melting totems of an old order; Jess's Play-doh figures, the children of a frightening urban future that Clare can neither come to terms with nor understand.

Jess will be one of Clare's failures. By the end of the speech we should understand why.

Hot strong sunlight.

Clare *is standing by her desk, three Plasticine figures like misshapen dolls standing in a row on the desk. Two of them are dressed in clothes, bits of old denim, etc., one of them is still wrapped up in dirty newspaper, completely covered.* **Clare** *faces us.*

Clare I came in a few days ago – and these squat little figures were waiting for me . . . wrapped up in newspaper, standing in a line on my desk.
They are in fact rather sturdily made, out of grubby Play-doh. Later that day Jess turned up, for an appointment. Bang on time as always.

She begins to unwrap third Plasticine figure.

(*As Jess.*) I see you've only unwrapped two of them – what are you trying to tell me? . . . they're no good?

By the way, what did you think of Marble Arch? – Best one yet, wasn't it?
Did I tell you, when I dropped it off, I met your partner, I really hate using that fucking word – I expect *you* do too . . . But you probably *have* to use it, don't you! Anyway, I met your 'partner', your boyfriend, your bloke – he's just right for you, isn't he – a bit shaggy, really calm and soothing, but quite funny . . . in a laid-back way. And he was really interested in my models. Yes!

Third figure coming out of newspaper.

And when I've told you about *these* – you'll want them on your mantelpiece, at home. You will!

Moving, holding the figure.

You see, I thought, let's look at this place – like the tourists do. See the city as they see it.

So first – we've got to call the policemen 'Bobbies' (*Pronouncing it with ludicrous American/Cockney accent.*) – the only people to use the word BOBBIES are Americans – like they say, 'Where are your cute London BOBBIES . . .?' (*She smiles.*) And you don't know what the fuck they're talking about . . .

And the second thing – YOU HAVE TO GO TO MADAME TUSSAUD'S. Oh yes . . . ! You know, the wax museum.

Because every time you pass there, it doesn't matter what day of the year it is – there's a truly FUCKING ENORMOUS QUEUE. Have you noticed that? – There is ALWAYS a queue. *All tourists.*

And for that reason – nobody that actually *lives* in London has been inside that wax museum for years and years and years . . . ! Anything could be going on in there, couldn't it!?

So – *I* went inside. I did. Just sneaked round the front of the queue, it was dead easy.

And you know what I saw . . . ? It was a very hot day . . . And all these models, the wax models, they were beginning to MELT.

The Prime Minister had shrunk a bit, one ear had run down the side of his chin . . . Prince Charles's face was sort of sinking into his chest, so the top was just one big misshapen ball, and the American President – he was going at the waist, and one of his legs was melting smaller, and curling round, so it was like a little tail.

No point you looking like that – you haven't been in the BLOODY PLACE, have you? . . . since you were ten probably! So you have no idea what's happening there . . . so shut up!

And I thought – stuff all these politicians and 'Pop Performers' . . . ! They should have a room, about my age group, about the FUTURE. Yeah. You know the 'Football fan of the future' with his machine gun held next to his football scarf, that sort of thing, and the 'Schoolkid of the future', with her porno virtual reality goggles for when she's playing in the playground.

So there we are – (*She lines up the three figures.*) that's who they are.

The funny thing is – you're ever so cool when I show you these things, you think that'll stop me bringing them to you . . . make us talk deeply instead – about my *insides*. But it just makes me bring them all the more.

My Mother Said I Never Should
by Charlotte Keatley

This play is about the difficult relationships between mothers and daughters. It shifts backwards and forwards between 1905 and 1987. The lives of four generations of women – their loves, expectations and choices – are set against the huge social changes of the twentieth century.

In this scene we are in 1987. Jackie is in her mid-thirties. She runs an art gallery in Manchester. Life is a success, but at its heart there is a painful secret. In the early seventies, at the age of nineteen, Jackie gave birth to an illegitimate daughter, Rosie. The demands of single parenthood were too much after Rosie's father moved up in the world with another woman, and under pressure from her mother, she gave Rosie up. Rosie was brought up by grandparents, Margaret and Ken. As Jackie drops in and out of family life, Rosie thinks she is her big sister.

In this scene Margaret has just died of cancer. Jackie, busy as ever, arrives at the hospital too late to see her. While sorting through Margaret's papers, teenage Rosie finds her birth certificate and the cat is out of the bag. As Rosie vents her feelings, Jackie is forced to justify the lie she has been living for the last fifteen years.

Short sentences punctuated by pauses and silences, bursts of anger and overemphasis, expose how difficult this is for Jackie. How can you tell your daughter that you gave her away? Jackie has just lost her own mother and wasn't there for her. Now her relationship with her daughter is at stake. Guilt and grief jostle for precedence as she offers this fractured explanation for what she did. She has clearly been lying to herself as much as to Rosie by hanging on to the myth that Rosie's father loved them. The glimpse into his trendy career and life-style gives us an inkling of Jackie's own aspirations and values. The truth is that however much she loves Rosie, there is no escape from that determining decision to give her up. 'You wanted your own life more than you wanted mine' accuses Rosie. However she presents her case, that's the bottom line and she knows it. Lonely, knowing what she has missed, Jackie is asking Rosie for a second chance. But is it too late?

Jackie How dare you! (*Goes to hit* **Rosie** *but cannot.*) You're at the centre of everything I do! (*Slight pause.*) Mummy treated me as though I'd simply fallen over and cut my knee – picked me up and said you'll be all right now, it won't show much. She wanted to make it all better. (*Quiet.*) . . . She was the one who wanted it kept secret . . . I WANTED you, Rosie. (*Angry.*) For the first time in my life I took care of myself – refused joints, did exercises, went to the clinic. (*Pause.*) 'It's a girl.' (*Smiles irresistibly.*) – After you'd gone I tried to lose that memory. (*Pause. Effort.*) Graham . . . your father. (*Silence.*) He couldn't be there the day you were born, he had to be in Liverpool. He was married. (*Emphatic.*) He loved me, he loved you, you must believe that! (*Pause.*) He said he'd leave his wife, but I knew he wouldn't; there were two children, the youngest was only four . . . we'd agreed, separate lives, I wanted to bring you up. He sent money. (*Pause.*) I took you to Lyme Park one day, I saw them together, across the lake, he was buying them ice creams, his wife was taking a photo. I think they live in Leeds now, I saw his name in the *Guardian* last year, an article about his photographs . . . (*Pause.*) It was a very cold winter after you were born. There were power cuts. I couldn't keep the room warm; there were no lights in the tower blocks; I knew he had an open fire, it was trendy; so we took a bus to Didsbury, big gardens, pine kitchens, made a change from concrete. I rang the bell. (*Stops.*) A Punjabi man answered, said he was sorry . . . they'd moved. By the time we got back to Mosside it was dark, the lift wasn't working – (*Stops.*) That was the night I phoned Mummy. (*Difficult.*) Asked her. (*Pause.*) I tried! I couldn't do it, Rosie. (*Pause.*) It doesn't matter how much you succeed afterwards, if you've failed once. (*Pause.*) After you'd gone . . . I kept waking in the night to feed you . . . A week . . . in the flat . . . Then I went back to art school. Sandra and Hugh thought I was inhuman. I remember the books that came out that winter – how to succeed as a single working mother – fairy tales! (*Pause.*) Sandra and Hugh have a family now. Quite a few of my friends do. (*Pause.*) I could give you everything now. Rosie? . . .

Wiping My Mother's Arse *by Iain Heggie*

Kath is in her early thirties, a feisty working-class single mum of teenage boys. A survivor. She sees life as it suits her to see it, her attitudes and values shaped by an Oprah Winfrey-type chat show. Her first husband battered her so she is cautious about boyfriend Derek who is forty plus, still unemployed and a bit of a mystery. However, he *does* have a job and a new house with garage and garden, so from Kath's point of view, he's a good bet.

In this very black comedy, Derek takes Kath to a nursing home to meet his senile mother, Andrene. But Kath discovers more than she bargained for when Derek's sado-masochistic relationship with Andrene's male care assistant comes to light and she finds he is not only unemployed but has stolen Andrene's money to buy his house as well.

In this scene she has taken destiny into her own hands and vengefully reported care assistant Larry (who has been on the fiddle in a minor way) to the head of the nursing home, Rosemary. Consequently, Larry is suspended. Here she reports her conversation with the head of the nursing home to Derek. The subtext might be, 'See, I'm not afraid to speak my mind! I told her what's what!', 'I don't care how important she thinks she is!', 'You've done nothing to be ashamed of. They are the guilty ones.' Notice the foul language and regular use of Rosemary's name and the effect that has. It demotes Rosemary's authority. Is this an accurate account of events I wonder? How much of it is for effect? After all, to acknowledge Derek's 'shortcomings' would be to scupper her game plan. Kath is actually prepared to take Derek on any terms and reinterprets events accordingly. She needs security and love. 'Denial' is her middle name.

You should be aware of, but not play Kath's agenda. Kath is not sufficiently self-aware to understand it herself.

Kath I did. I did if that's all you're worried about. I got Larry suspended. Well, I walked into her office, I did. I walked into Rosemary's shithole office and I said: 'Right, Rosemary, have you found out where Mrs MacAvennie's money's gone yet?' So she said: 'Well, I've just got through to the opticians.' So I said: 'And what did the opticians say, Rosemary?' She said: 'They said: "They have no record of Mrs MacAvennie buying 33 pairs of glasses in the last year." ' So I said: 'Well, that's no surprise to me, Rosemary. So what I want to know is why didn't you bloody notice all these requests for money for Mrs MacAvennie's glasses?' So she said: 'I'm very short-staffed and overworked so it's hard to keep track of every little detail.' So I said: 'You're not bloody overworked, Rosemary. You're just bloody inefficient. Look at the state of your office, for God's sake. My boys' bedrooms are tidier than this shithole.' She said: 'I'm very sorry.' I said: 'It's no good being sorry, Rosemary. What are you going to do about it?' She said: 'I'll phone head office and see what they want me to do.' I said: 'Sod that, Rosemary. You've got an old pervert down there fiddling money off your patients and you want to phone head bloody office.' And not only that, also he ruined your young life. He did. Till you had the sheer courage to get away. Can't have people like that fiddling about with your mother's parts! So I said to Rosemary, I said: 'Rosemary, get off your fat lazy arse and get that pervert searched and out the building right now or I'll go to the papers and tell them your office is a slum, you've got the manners of a pig and you dress like a sad old worn-out whore.'

Sliding with Suzanne *by Judy Upton*

Suzanne is a working-class foster-mum in her thirties from North London. She is bright, promiscuous, drinks, smokes dope and parties – anything to 'keep the dark out'. Her self-esteem and expectations have reached rock bottom. Luka, her troubled sixteen-year-old foster-son, has run off so she heads down to her mother's in Brighton for some support.

Suzanne's relationship with Luka is difficult, each giving as good as they get, but they seem to need each other. As she says, 'Luka and me, we swear and spit and scream. We've got a lot to be pissed off about.' In this scene she has just got home after a one-night stand with a seventeen-year-old shop assistant to find Luka has come to Brighton to find her. It's not clear which one of them has run away. Violence, recrimination and verbal abuse ensue.

In this speech Suzanne tells her mother how dreadful her life is, as if her 'shit' existence gives her an excuse for her behaviour. She wants help. Her language is vulgar and colourful, designed to shock Mum into some understanding of her situation. She can't get a decent place to live because she has no money. If she gets a low-paid job, she loses her benefits, is sexually harassed by her boss and isn't around for Luka. If she cuts her hours then she can't earn enough to make it worth her while. She's caught in the archetypal poverty trap. She wants a new start but can't see any way to achieve it. It's all pretty hopeless. She is in the frame of mind where nothing anyone says will make her see things differently.

Suzanne Well off! Why don't you ever listen to yourself, Mum? What do you mean, I should move? What am I supposed to do? Go down to the estate agency and say, 'Yeah, I'll have that one – the nice semi, with conservatory and reception rooms.' What the fuck's a reception room? I event went and got a job, Mum. You'd think I'd have learnt by now, wouldn't you? Course I lost my benefits, and no contract, no minimum wage, but what use are fucking A levels anyway? So there I am in a City coffee bar, making coffees, all kinds of bloody coffees – as quick as possible. And you've got to make them just right – just a drop too much milk and a macchiato becomes a latte and you can bet your life the customer's gonna give you hell. First day I scald my wrist so bad the skin just peeled off like it was plaster. The supervisor says I'm working too slow, starts standing right behind me . . . and pressing his fucking little dick against my arse. I tell him he's looking to get a Premium Expresso burning his beans. And if it wasn't him, it was the hordes of City tossers, trying to tug my thong every time I reached over to wipe a table. But I put up with the verbal, the groping cos I needed the money, needed to move from that shitty flat. Then Joanna says Luka's not going to school. 'Maybe you should try to be there for him a little more', or 'Maybe his needs don't fit in with your new career.' 'Career', yeah that was their word – my coffee-making career. So I cut down my hours, and then it wasn't worth the tube fare in.

Jesus Hopped the 'A' Train
by Stephen Adly Guirgis

This gritty play takes place in a high-security New York gaol on Rikers Island where brutality, psychological torture and racism prevail.

Mary Jane is a young attorney, a New Yorker of Italian Irish descent. She's been defence lawyer for Angel Cruz, a defiant young Puerto Rican on trial for the attempted murder of the Reverend Kim, a suspect cult leader. Angel's best friend had been recruited by Kim to the Jehovah's Witnesses. Angel had seen too many people from the ghetto disappear down this path and reacted by shooting the Reverend 'in the ass'. When the Reverend unexpectedly dies of his injuries, Angel is convicted of murder despite Mary Jane's best efforts to save him.

Mary Jane is talking directly to the audience, using it as a sounding board for her story.

Mary Jane's upbringing is poor, but unlike Angel she had opportunities which enabled her to climb out of her class. She is tough, driven, bright, and anarchic – a liberal with a strong sense of 'fair play' who has not lost touch with her roots. She's the only character in the play not directly involved in the brutal criminal justice system.

Why did she continue to defend Angel even when she no longer had any obligation to do so and suspected he was 'guilty as charged'? That's the irony of Mary Jane's position. Yet something about Angel's story and the expression on his face touched her, stirring childhood memories of a school dance when her father attacked someone. Mortifying? Inappropriate? Yes. Nevertheless, Mary Jane relates to her dad's outburst in the same way that she can relate to Angel's attack on Kim. The rational lawyer knows you can't go round shooting people or stabbing them with forks, but another part of her applauds the fact that they have defended their own. It's this tension that drives the speech. Angel is born on the wrong side of the tracks, just like her own family. Is it this that makes her stick with the case although she knows it is a hopeless cause?

Mary Jane Angel Cruz had said: 'All I did was shoot him in the ass'
. . . There was something so juvenile about that, obviously, but, for
me, although I wasn't aware of it at the time, there was also
something familiar and . . . nostalgic . . . When I was fifteen, there
had been this Father/Daughter Dance at the Elite Private Girls'
School in Manhattan that I went to as a charity case-slash-financial
aid recipient. My mother had, wisely, arranged for her brother,
Uncle Mikey, to take me to the Dance, but at the last minute, my
father decided that him not escorting me himself might be one of
those things that might scar me in later life – so – me and my father
left our two-family house in Sunnyside that evening; me in a dress
my parents couldn't afford, and my dad in his Irish All Purpose
Navy Blue Suit with a pair of black socks we had convinced him to
borrow from the neighbors . . . When we got inside the ballroom, I
took a quick look around and became instantly embarrassed to the
point of humiliation by the fact that my dad was the only father on
the Upper East Side that night whose suit pants didn't have cuffs.
But within an hour, everyone was calling him 'Danny', even the
Headmistress, who hadn't called me anything but 'Miss Hanrahan'
in three years. And he was dancing, and chatting. And he had even
stuck by the agreed-upon two-beer rule, or so I thought . . . At some
point in the evening, one of the other fathers made an off-hand
comment that my father took exception to; a heated discussion
ensued, and my father ended up stabbing the guy with a dessert
fork, breaking the skin . . . What the guy had said was unimportant;
actually, what he said was, he was reminiscing about where he had
grown up as a kid and he remarked that: 'It used to be a good
neighborhood, you know, white, now, forget it, I went back there
last month, it's half white, the rest: blacks and Italians.' My mom's
Italian. EMS was called, and the dance? – Well, let's just say the
stabbing concluded the dancing portion of the evening . . . My
father's justification for the assault, after explaining how he didn't
immediately attack him, and how he had given the 'rich jerk' ample
opportunity to apologize, and how he won't tolerate a bigot no
matter where he is, and: 'What if your mom or "Rasheed from the
Deli" had been there?', and how he still doesn't understand why I

need to go to that stuck-up school anyway. In the end, what he finally said was: 'It was just a fork' . . . And he said it, I've now come to realize, with just that same look of incredulousness on his face that Angel Cruz had on his . . . as if the whole world was crazy and he was the only sane one . . . I hated my dad for the whole mortifying incident, but the dysfunctional side of me was proud of him – actually, I'm still kind of proud of him – and I'm not convinced that there's something wrong with me for feeling that. I had no idea why Angel Cruz had 'just shot him in the ass' but I felt something – something – and I needed to know what it was. And even though I was no longer obligated to him as his counsel, and despite the fact that the rational side of my brain was very much convinced that he had, in fact, attempted to murder Reverend Kim, and, yes, of course, even if he hadn't literally attempted murder, you still can't run around shooting people just like you can't go around stabbing people with dessert forks, I know all that, but I gotta admit, that somewhere inside of me, and I don't know if it's the good side, or the side that I saw a therapist twice a week and went to ACOA meetings for, but somewhere inside of me is a place that believes that sometimes you can do these things, or at least, somebody can, or, should, and that one man's neurotic is another man's hero, and who, ultimately, can say which one's which with any real certainty at all? . . .

Perfect Strangers *by Stephen Poliakoff*

When members of an old English family are brought together for a reunion in one of London's grand hotels a genealogical minefield is exposed. As they 'pursue their pedigrees' a series of family snapshots become a source of some disturbing revelations. The piece is taken from a screenplay – but this should not affect how you play it for a theatre audition.

Alice, a beautifully-turned-out woman in her middle years is the hostess of the event. She is radiant, authoritative and self-contained. In the writer's description, 'there is something both modern and period about her. She is modern in her bright intelligent eyes, but her careful elegance has an old-fashioned quality.' She has a vulnerable quality too, and for many years has been carrying a burden of guilt, which she confesses in this speech.

Rebecca, Charles and Richard, the three siblings in Alice's story, were victims of neglectful parenting and were consequently semi-adopted by Alice, their young and interesting aunt, who encouraged them and gave them love. Richard, the middle child, was the most fun, the most imaginative of the three but when he began to display more and more symptoms of an undiagnosed mental illness, he was surreptitiously and incrementally marginalised by the others. The picnic she describes is the final straw in their callous disregard for his feelings.

Her delivery of the story is careful and restrained but told with such meticulous detail that we revisit the scene with her. Nothing has been forgotten of that dreadful day. We glimpse her pain but it simply wouldn't do for a woman like Alice to indulge it. It is the almost factual delivery that gives the speech its power and Richard's suicide its shocking impact.

———————————

Alice We were having Sunday lunch at my house in Buckinghamshire. My husband Robert had only been dead a couple of years . . . And I really loved to see Rebecca and Charles. And we were sitting having coffee after lunch . . . it was a perfect summer afternoon . . . and suddenly we looked up and there was Richard, coming across the lawn. I'll never forget it. He was carrying this rather nice picnic basket. And he says, 'We must have a picnic.' And we say we can't . . . we've just had lunch . . . and he says, 'Oh, come on, I've found the perfect spot and I've bought the perfect picnic.'

And so we follow him, first to the bottom of the garden . . . 'Isn't this the perfect spot?' he says.

And just as we've all sat down, and he's started unpacking the basket, he says, 'No, this isn't the spot. This spot isn't good enough.'

And we get up . . . and he says, 'No, the perfect spot is just over here.' And we move over to the beginning of the wood, and we settle in the shade under a tree. And he says, 'This is much more like the perfect spot.' And then the same thing happens again. We've sat down, he begins to unpack the picnic, and then he decides the spot isn't good enough, and then we're all off, and again and again this happens.

And we get further into the wood, deeper and deeper. And then at last he says, 'This is it . . . this is the perfect spot.' And we've ended up by some disgusting pipes, a drainage system.

And we just can't follow him down there by the pipes. I can't bear the idea of sitting there with him saying, 'Do you understand the significance of the noise these pipes are making?' None of us could cope sitting there that day and that happening.

And we lose him. We let him unpack the picnic, and we leave him there . . . We scramble away . . . we can hear him calling . . . He's completely surprised we've left him there . . . And then because we know he'll follow us straight back to the house . . . We get into the car and drive round and round in circles for hours, longing for him not to be there when we get back . . .

She is nearly in tears, but then the moment passes.

He wasn't, in fact. He wasn't there when we got back. And it was not the only time we did something like that, not by any means . . .

And then one day he walked on to a railway line and was hit by a train.

Bailegangaire *by Tom Murphy*

The scene is the kitchen of Mommo's run-down house in the deprived west of Ireland. It is 1984.

Dolly is a local woman, aged thirty-nine, promiscuous, attractive in a blowsy sort of way – 'like her name, dolled up, gaudy rural fashion'. Before marrying her violent husband Stephen and having several children, Dolly spent ten years as carer to her grandmother, Mommo, resentfully overseeing her decline into senile dementia. Mommo had watched Dolly's husband beat and abuse her without lifting a finger to help or opening her mouth in protest.

Now Dolly is pregnant by one of her random lovers, a condition that is proving difficult to conceal. She is terrified her largely absent husband will find out. Older sister Mary (top of the class with a string of nursing qualifications) has come home to take over Mommo's care and find resolution to some painful family issues.

In this scene Dolly comes round to Mommo's with a bottle of vodka. She is drunk and has something on her mind. She has a proposition to put to Mary. In an incongruous solution to the muddle of her life, she offers Mary her unborn child. Mary finds the suggestion ludicrous and in an attempt to mollify Dolly, acknowledges that her own life is an equal failure. Her admission triggers this tirade.

The speech is full of rapid emotional shifts and short dislocated sentences. It is both accusation and appeal, designed to hurt and shock her sensitive sister into understanding. But defiant as Dolly seems, remember she is a victim – a battered wife, locked in a loveless marriage by children, lack of education, economic dependence and the moral straitjacket of the Catholic Church. Her life is a mess and there is no escaping it. Everything about her – clothes, attitudes, sexual behaviour – is a 'front', a thin disguise for her unhappiness. It is her own life and circumstances, not Mary, that are the real target for this outburst.

Dolly No! No! You had it easy! – You had it – You had – I had – I had ten! – I had a lifetime! – A lifetime! – Here with myself, doin' her every bidding, listenin' to her seafóid (*rambling*) gettin' worse till I didn't know where I was! – Pissin' in the bed beside me – I had a lifetime! Then the great Stephen – the surprise of it! comes coortin'! Never once felt any – real – warmth from him – what's wrong with him? – but he's my rescuer, my saviour. But then, no rhyme or reason to it – He could've got a job at that plant, but he couldn't wait to be gone either! Then waitin' for the hero, my rescuer, the sun shining out of his eighty-five-pounds-a-week arse, to come home at Christmas. No interest in me – oh, he used me! – or in children, or the rotten thatch or the broken window, or Conor above moving in his fence from *this* side. I'm fightin' all the battles. Still fightin' the battles. And what d'yeh think he's doin' now this minute? Sittin' by the hearth in Coventry, is he? Last Christmas an' he was hardly off the bus, Old Sharp Eyes whisperin' into his ear about me. Oooo, but he waited. Jesus, how I hate him! Jesus, how I hate them! Men! Had his fun and games with me that night, *and* first thing in the morning. Even sat down to eat the hearty breakfast I made. Me thinkin', still no warmth, but maybe it's goin' to be okay. Oooo, but I should've known from *experience* about-the-great-up-standin'-Steph-en-evrabody's-fav-our-ite. Because, next thing he has me by the hair of the head, fistin' me down in the mouth. Old Sharp Eyes there, noddin' her head every time he struck an' struck an' kicked an' kicked an' pulled me round the house by the hair of the head. Jesus, men! (*Indicating the outdoors where she had her sex.*) You-think-I-enjoy? I-use-*them*! Jesus, hypocrisy! An' then, me left with my face like a balloon – you saw a lot of me last Christmas, didn't yeh? – my body black and blue, the street angel an' his religious mother – 'As true as Our Lady is in heaven now, darlin's' – over the road to visit you an' Mommo with a little present an' a happy an' a holy Christmas now darlin's an' blessed St-fuckin'-Jude an' all the rest of them flyin' about for themselves up there.

Peggy For You *by Alan Plater*

Peggy Ramsay was a real-life play agent who has become as famous as many of the writers she represented. She was a legend in her own lifetime. **Peggy For You** (a reference to phone calls beginning thus) takes place in Peggy's chaotic offices in St Martin's Lane on an eventful but imaginary day in the late sixties when one young talent is recruited, another resigns in disgust, and yet another commits suicide.

Peggy, Queen Bee of a literary universe, is in the prime of middle age. She is elegant, dedicated, charismatic, intelligent, capricious, articulate, indiscreet, witty, imperious, rude, iconoclastic, anarchic, inspiring, hard as nails, disinterested in money and passionate about art. She is a powerful figure on the theatrical scene and loud! The floor is littered with the names she drops – all known to her personally. It is a brave man who stands up to Peggy Ramsay.

This speech comes at the beginning of the play. Peggy has just stood bail for one of her renegade clients and has, not untypically, arrived at the office at crack of dawn. It consists of two telephone conversations, the first with one of her clients, the other with her live-in partner, Bill. As with all stage telephone conversations you need to have a clear idea of what your character is hearing at the other end of the line. Fill in the writer's dots! How does her client respond to being woken up? How does he take 'the lash' of her criticism? What sort of relationship do they have? The conversation at Peggy's end is littered with 'darlings', theatrical references and high-flown superlatives. The real Peggy Ramsay worked in the theatre in her younger days, and can't you tell! The conversation with Bill, on the other hand, has a very different flavour. The nature of this relationship is clear too. Peggy is definitely in the driving seat.

Peggy Ramsay was Alan Plater's own agent for thirty years. You can do no better than go to his vivid introduction to the play to find more helpful information about her life and character. Then you must make her your own.

Peggy *lies on the chaise longue in her office reading a script. There are two piles – To Read and Read. Both are enormous. She finishes the one she's reading and reaches for the telephone, which is lying on the floor nearby. With some difficulty she dials the numbers, squinting over her glasses to read the number on the script. She waits, then:*

Peggy I'm sorry, darling, have I stopped you working? (. . .) I've what? I've stopped you sleeping? I've woken you up? Oh my God, what time is it? (. . .) You must forgive me, I haven't actually been to bed, I came here directly from the police station. (. . .) I was bailing out a client, it's terribly interesting, have you ever been to a police station? You should. Everybody should. What? (. . .) Of course I've read your play. That's why I'm ringing you, but you tell me you're asleep, do you really want to talk about it? (. . .) As you wish, I am totally at your service. Well, I think it's wonderfully written, but that's really the problem. You should write a novel, get all that fine writing out of your system. Everybody writes elegies, darling, they're terribly easy to do. I blame Chekhov. That's the trouble with geniuses, they can be thrilling but they do tend to fuck up their followers. (. . .) Of course we can get it on somewhere, darling, if you really want me to. I could probably bully the Royal Court into doing it, but are you sure that's wise? There's an awful lot of gazing into the middle distance and dreaming of Moscow, and do we really give a shit? (*Listens, laughs.*) What a wonderful idea! Go to Moscow and get the elegies out of your system. Why don't you do that? But you must promise to send a postcard of Lenin's tomb to the office. Now go back to sleep, little one. Flights of angels. Byee!

She hangs up, picks up another script, starts to read.

The telephone rings. She answers it.

Margaret Ramsay Limited. (. . .) Of course I'm here, Bill, where else is there to go at this time in the morning? (. . .) It all took a little time so I decided not to bother coming home. I stole my way into the office to read some plays before the madness descends. (. . .) It was totally delightful. I met this sweet chief superintendent who adores Galsworthy, can you imagine? (. . .) What? Oh, they arrested comrade David for singing filthy songs outside the French Embassy. (. . .) Apparently he was celebrating Alfred Jarry's birthday and he got this sudden urge to storm somewhere. Have you ever stood bail for anybody? (. . .) It's surprisingly easy, and it doesn't actually cost you anything, you simply promise to stump up if your criminal tries to run away. Which is highly unlikely, since David's generally too pissed to walk, let alone run. (. . .) What? I don't know, I expect I'll be home at the usual time. (. . .) Am I? Well, if you say I'm going to the National I suppose I must be. There's a diary somewhere in the office but Tessa seems to have lost it again. So I'll be home at whatever the usual time is when I've been to the National. Goodbye, dear.

She hangs up, resumes reading the next script in the pile.

Fashion *by Doug Lucie*

The dubious relationship between politics and the advertising industry is the theme of Doug Lucie's snarling drama. The action takes place in the mid-1980s in the run-up to a general election.

Amanda is a tabloid journalist working for the Maxwell Group. 'It's a dirty job, but someone's got to do it.' She used to write for *New Left Review*. She is in her forties, attractive, high-flying, hard-bitten and articulate. She is married to Stuart, a brilliant but alcoholic left-wing film director. She is having an affair with Paul Cash, the unprincipled MD of Cash Creative Consultancy who has been pitching for the Conservative account and the chance to produce the next series of Conservative Party Political Broadcasts. Spurred by guilt and enlightened self-interest, Cash has hired Stuart, whose career is on the skids, to help him 'make his pitch'. As a result the Consultancy have landed the account, helped deliver another Tory victory and facilitated the election of a dreadful narrow-minded, self-styled 'Thatcher clone' from the Shires.

In this scene they are celebrating with champagne in Cash's office. Amanda has been knocking it back. When Eric Bright, a former Labour MP who has rejected both Party and working-class origins in favour of a well-heeled media career delivers a full-frontal attack on socialism, it gets right up Amanda's nose. Bright, now an apologist for the Thatcher government, has been helping the Consultancy groom Tory candidates for office.

This speech is a scathing indictment of his hypocrisy. Amanda doesn't pull her punches. She's really letting him have it. Champagne has loosened her tongue and she's taken the floor. Her aim is to debunk him, knock him off his high and mighty pedestal. Look how often she uses the word 'little'. The tone of the speech is scathing and derisory. You can't help thinking that she really does care about something, even if it has got subverted along the way. She is not just sickened by Bright and his kind, but by the whole, distasteful, self-serving political scene.

Amanda You, of course, would know all about the people and what they want. With your intimate knowledge of them. From your Channel Island tax haven and your pied-à-terre in Bloomsbury. I think, if you were to be completely honest, you'd have to say that you're making educated guesses based on self-interest and innate prejudice. Oh, I know those are the perfect qualifications for membership of your little club, the Sunday pontificators, but they're sod all to do with the real world. God, we used to go to church to be preached at and told what was wrong and what was right. Now we just open the paper and up pops the pulpit and there's little Eric Bright telling it how it really is. You and your little chums, all barking away together. D'you know what you make me think of when you're on the soap box? D'you know what I see? I see good lunches. Fine wine. And great fat cigars. (*Beat.*) You're the self-appointed loudhailers for a government that's turned this country into a land fit for Rupert Murdoch. It amazes me that you'll all give credence to this dim-witted country cow, who, by some freak of nature, is now a Member of Parliament, for Christ's sake, and yet you pour all the shit you can on the idea, just the idea, of socialism. Well, it's not the people who are scared of socialism, it's you. Because it would drop your lovely lunch in your lap, and stick your great fat cigar up your arse. You want politics, sister? I'll give you politics. Not my husband's soggy labourist crap. That's just Tory paternalism with a collectivist face. Thanks to their silly soft-centre deference we still live in one of the most class-ridden, tradition-bound societies in the modern world.

The Rise and Fall of Little Voice
by Jim Cartwright

Mari is a widow in her forties. She lives with her agora-
phobic and largely silent daughter, LV (Little Voice of the
title), whom she dominates and despises. LV spends most of
her time in her room listening to her absent father's record
collection and imitating the singers with amazing verisi-
militude. Mari is northern, boozy, blowsy, loud-mouthed,
combustible, raunchy, working-class, selfish, and sexually
'past her sell-by date'. But that doesn't stop her trying to
'cop off'. She's mutton dressed up as lamb. She speaks
before her mind's in gear.

Dressed for the sexual 'kill' she has just got back from a
nightclub to find her house a burnt-out husk. She thinks LV
has set fire to it. Full of drink she surveys the embers. It's a
potent metaphor for burnt-out youth and the guttering of
sexual power.

This is rock bottom. Her house is gone. She has been
deserted by Ray Say, a seedy nightclub owner, whom she
saw as her last chance of happiness. She's lost everything.
The speech is littered with the imagery of a gutted life.

Language rattles out of her, aggressive, uncensored with
no thought for the damage she might inflict. She's never
been much of a mother to the sensitive and vulnerable LV.
Now the things she says are cruel and indefensible. But the
lid is off, the game is up and like a trapped rat she attacks
and goes for the jugular. All those years of feeling excluded
from the relationship between LV and her father, her
inadequacy in the face of their shared interests, her jealousy
of LV's talent and the frustration at being trapped in a life
she feels she's too good for explode out of her in an
impotent tirade of self-pity, defiance and blame, revealing
her as a mean-spirited, disappointed, jealous woman.

The speech comes at the end of the play and drives the
mouse-like LV to deliver her own terrible indictment of her
mother before she understandably abandons her too.

Mari I'm now in the carcass of my house, a smoked ham. I can't start again. What's the next move? I'm too beat for a man, really I ask you. I've been jumping the coals for years, now I've finally fallen in. Nobody wants the burnt bits, have you noticed? They love a blazing bint but when the flames have gone who wants the char? Well, some might say I've got what I deserve. But that's the problem, I've never had what I deserved. I was more than this dump I had to live in. In fact, my energy itself could have burnt this place down years ago, four times over with fireworks for ever. I was more than what I married. Your father, your father kissing me with his parlour lips. I had health and breasts and legs. I strode. When I got behind your pram I propelled it about a hundred miles an hour. The air was full of the sound of wolf whistles, deafening. He was shambling somewhere behind, a beanpole Chaplin. But you, you were always his. It was always you and him, you and him all the time, doing quiet things, heads bent together, listening to the records. Driving me mad, my energy could have burnt this house down four times over, and you two tilted into books, listening to the radio shows, playing board games in front of the fire. Fuck it. And now I'm dancing on my own grave and it's a roasting tin. My house gutted, my last possession gone. My last chance charred. Look at me up to my ankles in char. (*Looking at the thick soot over the floor.*) In fact, this is my soul leaking over the floor here, soot itself. I'm going to scoop handfuls up and spread it over you. Your head, you see, was the match head to this. (*Indicating everything.*) What's up, cat got your tongue?

The Beauty Queen of Leenane
by Martin McDonagh

The play is set in a rural cottage in the west of Ireland, the home of a vitriolic old woman, Mag, and her daughter, Maureen. Maureen is plain, uneducated, aged forty, and up to this point, a virgin. She is Mag's reluctant carer, trapped in rural Ireland without any escape route except a man. Mag's ceaseless demands, dissatisfaction and evil tongue have blighted Maureen's life.

In this scene Maureen has found love and sex and is flaunting it in front of her mother out of sheer 'badness'. She is in her underwear. Her behaviour is unbalanced and sexually explicit. It embarrasses her lover, Pato, and enrages her mother. In a destructive 'tit for tat' outburst Mag attempts to spoil Maureen's happiness by revealing to Pato that Maureen has spent time in an English mental institution. Maureen is shocked and angered by her mother's revelation. She feels defensive and ashamed. The stigma of mental illness still dogs her and she's desperate it shouldn't spoil her chances with Pato. She was young she explains, away from home, doing a soul-destroying cleaning job, the victim of verbal abuse and English racism. She had no friends, except for one, and when she moved on, everything got too much. Her agenda is to make Pato understand that her instability is a thing of the past. For Maureen there is so much at stake. How else will she escape her life? But the more she tries to justify her breakdown, the more she reveals herself as an emotionally fragile woman, unable to cope with life's pressures.

Maureen (*quietly*) It's true I was in a home there a while, now, after a bit of a breakdown I had. Years ago, this is. In England I was, this happened. Cleaning work. When I was twenty-five. Me first time over. Me only time over. Me sister had just got married, me other sister just about to. Over in Leeds I was, cleaning offices. Bogs. A whole group of us, only them were all English. 'Ya oul backward Paddy fecking . . . The fecking pig's-backside face on ya.' The first time out of Connemara this was I'd been. 'Get back to that backward fecking bog of yours or whatever hole it was you drug yourself out of.' Half of the swearing I didn't even understand. I had to have a black woman explain it to me. Trinidad she was from. They'd have a go at her too, but she'd just laugh. This big face she had, this big oul smile. And photos of Trinidad she'd show me, and 'What the hell have you left there for?' I'd say. 'To come to this place, cleaning shite?' And a calendar with a picture of Connemara on I showed her one day, and 'What the hell have you left there for?' she said back to me. 'To come to this place . . .' (*Pause.*) But she moved to London then, her husband was dying. And after that it all just got to me.

Never Land *by Phyllis Nagy*

Anne Joubert is a beautiful middle-aged Frenchwoman, married to her childhood sweetheart, Henri, to whom she is sexually unresponsive. She is alcoholic.

Their house stands on a beautiful hillside in southern France. It is as unstable as the relationships within it. Henri, a passionate Anglophile, has always dreamt of starting a new life in England. At his behest Anne and their dependent daughter Elisabeth speak nothing but English, which they articulate in perfect RP.

All their married life Henri has pursued hair-brained initiatives, which have come to nothing. Only a job in the local perfumery and the indulgence of his employer has enabled him to keep family and soul together. Now all prospects have foundered. Henri's dream prospect of managing a bookshop in Bristol has disintegrated and with it all hopes of ever being economically solvent. He has resigned his job at the perfumery and the family faces financial ruin.

In this final scene Henri and Elisabeth plan to put the family out of its misery. Henri is to shoot Elisabeth first. While they go outside to do it, Anne enters looking radiantly beautiful. She has the edgy energy of someone who hasn't slept for two days. She addresses the audience and carefully sets out the mangled remains of an earlier picnic – broken vessels, empty bottles, half-eaten food – as if nothing is broken or destroyed. It is emblematic of their shattered lives. Notice how her story slips into the present tense as she regresses to a 'never land' of the past – the halcyon days of meeting Henri, and falling in love in spite of his obvious inadequacies, her inability to 'conjugate' verbs easily presaging her inability to 'conjugate' in her marriage. Look how colour, light and sense are heightened in her rose-tinted reconstruction, It is as if she has insulated herself from reality in a magic sunlit bubble.

Even when the shotgun sounds in the garden she barely hesitates in her narrative. She is in total denial. The present is too terrible to contemplate. The past is another country and she was happy there. It is the only place left to inhabit.

Anne *enters. She is dressed in* **Henri**'s *robe. She is barefoot. Her hair is combed out neatly. And she is devastatingly beautiful. She carries a picnic basket. Throughout the following speech, she will open the basket and spread out its contents. They are half-eaten pieces of cheese, soiled linen, dirty silverware, empty wine bottles, chipped glasses and assorted debris of her daughter's earlier picnic. But* **Anne** *lays everything out as if it sparkles and shines.*

Anne (*addresses the audience*) I saw him in the distance as I started up the grassy path and the first thing that struck me was his hair, the colour of wild honey and strawberry jam. It sparkled and gleamed in the sunlight, so much so that as I sped down the stony path towards the brook opposite our house, my glasses caught a startling ray of light which I am certain bounced off his head and into my line of sight. I was struck blind and tumbled down down my body soft against the bumpy path and there he was, fumbling with a bunch of battered school books trying desperately to figure out how to offer me his hand. He never has properly figured it out. But he leaned across me when I needed him and so he takes me in his arms when I need him today. I don't know what this date shall lead to, and papa really doesn't care for him, thinks him shifty and shiftless. But he is shy and expects little of me and kisses me only when I ask to be kissed. He taught himself to read and me also when no teacher could be bothered to understand my reluctance to learn the rules of grammar or my reluctance to conjugate. His hands are warm to the touch and though I know my pulse should quicken in his presence though I never look at him and tremble with the anticipation of tracing the outline of his muscles with my forefinger though I wonder why it is he seems incapable of placing one foot in front of the other without stumbling I close my eyes and feel the heat of that single ray of glorious light from his hair piercing my vision and I know. He is the one. There has never been a question. We are learning English. Well. We are rather good at it already. We will marry soon though there is no hurry when there is so much time, time stretching out ahead of us like a map of happiness inviting us to plan yet farther routes. Today we go a-hunting. Papa says, but Anne, it is ludicrous to hunt foxes in this part of France. There are no foxes to be had. But Henri says we must practise hunting foxes. It's very English, he says. And I believe him. I love him when he speaks of England of opportunity of less small-minded nosiness of flat flat land as far as the eye can see. We will marry. Yes. but not now. First, we hunt.

A muffled shotgun blast is heard. It is absolutely startling, even though it is somewhat muted. **Anne** *hesitates before going on. It is clear she hears the shot and makes the decision to continue.*

I could have a handsomer man. I could have a richer man. And I am certain that out there somewhere is a man who will make my pulse race, my blood grow hot with desire. But it's a funny thing, this inability of mine to forget a simple act of kindness. His hand on my bleeding knee as he wraps his jacket around his knuckles and cleans my skin purifies my hurt and in the process ruins his chances. I know. In that instant I know Henri is the only man who will hoist the burden of me upon his shoulders and run with me all the way to the end. And that is worth . . . my fidelity. My complicity. In each of his endeavours. Isn't it?

Blue Murder *by Peter Nichols*

This is an intricately plotted farce set in the sixties. Its structure is rather like a set of Russian dolls – it's a play within a play within a play . . . The interface between fact and fiction offers a rich vein of comedy.

Act One or 'Foreign Bodies' takes us to 'Homes and Gardens' Shrewsbury where a young author struggles to write his first play. Act Two, 'A Game of Soldiers', takes place in Whitehall (literally a Whitehall farce!) where the same dreadful play (in which cyanide, dropped trousers, porn movies and gardening are all active ingredients), comes before the Censor.

Daphne is a middle-aged, not awfully good actress 'of the old school darling' who plays a stereotypical 'cor blimey, love a duck' tea lady of the same name in the play within the play within the . . . (The ins and outs of the plot are too complex to unpick here – you really will have to read it.) Daphne's very much 'to the manor born', but is still wearing her tea lady costume from her performance. All the actors have come out, guns blazing, about 'doubling up', the quality of the writing and the integrity of their characters. Sound familiar? This is Daphne's theme, although one can't help feeling that Daphne, the actress, is just as much a stereotype as Daphne the tea lady. Someone should tell Daphne that there are no small parts, only small actors.

Who runs the show – the writer, director or censor – is the serious theme at the heart of this rollicking satire on the world of theatre and its personnel.

Daphne Darling, d'you mind? I mean, you've been in this act from the start, while I've been stuck in the dressing room listening to all of you on the speaker. Very nearly finished my nephew's jumper. You know, I was in two minds about taking these parts, as Daphne was not much more than a spit and a cough in Act Two. Half an hour before she's seen at all, no sooner on than she's off again to fetch a biscuit. On again and it's off with the colonel's trousers. I mean off-stage. Then she stands here struck dumb while you all go whingeing on about the size of your parts. No, it's time I spoke. And, if I may say so, Nicholas dear, you've seriously undervalued the tea lady's potential. She alone embodies the continuing strain of earthy humour in English life. From the Wife of Bath in Chaucer through, say, Juliet's nurse and Doll Tearsheet, down to Hogarth and Rowlandson, till the Victorians finally gagged her and forced her to resort to the prudery of *double entendres* . . . at least while she's in the censor's office. And even here she's raised her husband's bawdry to an almost mythic level . . . God, such potential there! I know your point is that bourgeois playwrights have turned her sort into the comic servant, as a way of keeping them in their place. But, darling, I have to say you've quite failed to articulate it.

Good Fun *by Victoria Wood*

Betty is a door-to-door cosmetics saleswoman in her early fifties. Victoria Wood says she speaks with 'a concealed Lancashire accent', suggesting she puts on a bit of a voice for the job. She is carrying a large pink suitcase bulging with products. When she turns up at a northern arts centre, preparations for a fund-raising party for cystitis sufferers are under way. She only gets admitted because everyone thinks she is the drag artist for the cabaret.

We all know sales folk like Betty. They have their agenda, their pitch and their patter. Not hell or high water will distract them from it. Betty is Mrs Motormouth. She's done the sales training and got the T-shirt. She's pressing (but in a nice way), professional, proficient and convincing. A friendly approach littered with personal anecdotes and well-used one-liners soften her dedicated intention. 'No' is not in her vocabulary, and wouldn't you buy anything just to get rid of her?

The danger is to let the comedy run away with you rather than allow the situation to speak for itself. Victoria Wood's writing already heightens reality without any need to exaggerate it. The challenge is to breathe real life into Betty without any hint of caricature.

Although written in 'northern' English with a rather 'mumsy' feel, the piece should work for any actor over thirty-five with any accent. I have cut and edited it slightly so it works as a self-contained monologue.

A final tip – don't try and mime all the complex stage directions. The speech will work just as well without them.

Betty Now, first things first. Let me make it crystal clear that you are not obliged to purchase. (*Settling in.*) Though, obviously, one isn't trudging from door to door with a hereditary hip complaint for nothing. Now, may I use your table? Don't say no – use up too many of that little word, and you could find yourself with nothing to say in a sticky situation. (*Opens up a huge pink suitcase – displays huge racks of rows of bright pink cosmetics.*) Shall we start with you, dear? Are those tints natural? We'll give you the benefit of the doubt, though what they can do with henna these days is nobody's business. (*She dabs perfume on* **Lynne***'s wrist.*) We recommend this for a redhead. It's mainly musk, and let's face it, you never see a frigid polecat. And last? I should say so. I spilt some on my husband's gardening trousers the previous October, and he was still getting funny looks from the dustmen when they came round for their Christmas box. That smell will stay with you, don't you worry. Only £3.90 for the splash-on, and when it's empty, it converts into a salt pot. Now, I'm going to be a bit controversial now, I'll probably set you three girls at each other's throats – I'm going to tell you Powder Blusher is on the way out! You're stunned, aren't you? I was taken aback myself, when Mr McBurnie broke it to me. But these new pencils are marvellous because you can put it where you want it, which is half the battle. (*Dabs at* **Liz***'s face.*) Now blend that lightly yourself. I'm not one of these make-up ladies forever taking a poke at your cheekbones.

Dabbing at the girls' faces, bringing out eye shadow to put on their wrists while she speaks. In a complete flurry of compacts, lipsticks, etc., trying them on the girls, on herself, putting them back, etc.

(*To* **Liz***.*) Now, I don't know if you're troubled by sebum at all, but it will block your pores given half a chance, and I don't think you've been as thorough with a slice of cucumber as you might be, have you? I may sell commercial products, but I have to be fair. I have seen wonders done with Fuller's Earth and a couple of old teabags. So what I'm saying – What I'm saying, Liz, is this: if you do get a little black visitor, don't squeeze it – unless your hands are covered in a sterilised silk hanky, which, let's face it, chances are they won't be. Don't squeeze – cover it up with our push-up blemish concealer; three shades, fair, beige and tawny for those of us with the compulsory suntans, and don't they make good nurses? Now, we've a nice line in Zodiac powder compacts. We haven't a Taurus, but the Gemini's a pretty colour, don't you think. My son's on the cusp but you'd never know to look at him. (*To* **Lynne**.) Now, you're young enough to love a gimmick. (*Taking out some kind of stuffed toy with cosmetics inside it.*) Now, isn't he cute? And all the shades are matched – such a boon for the fashion-conscious colour-blind. These were Mr Thornton's idea originally, he really is a brilliant person, and kind! He conducts a choir of over two hundred agoraphobics, mainly sopranos for some reason. Such a shame, because they can never have an annual outing.

By now she is packing up a few things for each girl, taking it for granted they will buy them.

There's so many of them, it's a wonder they can all see his baton. Mr Thornton says he really needs one six-foot long with a red light on the end. So that's £1.28 for the blemish concealer, the compact is £3, now don't flinch, it's refillable, and Betty Bear, they claim they didn't call her after me, but I have my doubts, just £6.50.

(*Shuts case and relaxes.*) So, what goes on here? It looks very . . . happy-go-lucky.

The Architect *by David Greig*

Sheena, a community activist in her fifties lives on a neglected high-rise council estate in Edinburgh's docklands – ironically named Eden Court. Scottish, intelligent, passionate, insightful – she believes in 'people power'. She has been campaigning on behalf of the tenants for the dreadful blocks to be demolished.

High up on the balcony of her flat, she talks to Leo, the original architect of the estate whose idealism, like his buildings, is crumbling. From here they can see the site of another local scheme – also Leo's brainchild – which incorporates a refurbished Eden Court in the design. She needs Leo's support to change the plans. The pressure points of persuasion are subtle and oblique. Look how almost every sentence starts on a new line, giving a strong clue to her delivery. Each thought is weighed. She doesn't blame him. She mustn't alienate him. It matters too much. She must make him understand that times have changed – his vision for a model village in the sky has turned into a prison for its inhabitants. Sheena's point is irresistibly brought home by the bleak imagery of the flats as 'containers for people' abandoned on the dockside waiting to be shifted.

Look at the concise nature of the speech – the images are carefully chosen: the transformation of the economy of a city in less than thirty lines. Sheena must make Leo care – reactivate something he once believed in but now merely pays lip service to. As she shares her own original hopes and expectations for life on Eden Court she reaches out to the old Leo who believed that his vision could make a difference – who also had hopes and expectations for the tenants of Eden Court. Ironically, her passion and belief in the ability to change things are the very qualities that Leo has lost along the way. Sheena will be one of the instruments of his redemption.

Sheena You can see your new site, from here.

I've watched it. Watched the cranes pull it all up.

Watched the wrecking ball.

It looks pretty from a distance. The docks and everything.

The water in the background. It's pretty.

It looks nice with the sunset.

When I first lived here I watched the ships.

Watched the men loading and unloading.

Cars and crates of whisky, loads of coal and sacks of bananas.

I thought it was a privilege. Living above the docks.

Watching over the city's front door. And then the front door closed.

Containers.

You know the containers you put on ships, on lorries . . .

As soon as they invented containers there was no need for docks in the city centre. No need for dockers. A port and a motorway's all you need. The crane lifts the box out of the ship and on to the back of the truck. Done.

So the dockers and the sailors lost their jobs and you got yours . . . making museums and restaurants out of warehouses and whisky bonds.

Even the tarts moved inland.

All that got left here was people who were stuck.

Stuck in boxes on the dockside waiting to be picked up.

Hoping someone's going to stop for us and take us with them.

Ghost from a Perfect Place *by Philip Ridley*

The 'perfect place' of the title is the 'heyday' of the East End when the streets were 'kept clean' by the likes of the Kray Twins.

Torchie is sixty, but looks older. Life has taken its toll. She's a tough, unsentimental East Ender, a survivor. Her leg has been badly burnt in a fire so she walks painfully with a stick. The 'salt of the earth' some might say. She is cared for by her young granddaughter, Rio, who is a prostitute.

Now, twenty-five years on, Travis Flood, a legendary gangster, is back in town. He's come from America to publicise a book about his brutal reign. He has picked Rio up in the local graveyard. Rio 'services' her clients in Gran's flat but Travis has arrived early for his appointment and finds Torchie there. After all these years Torchie is still in awe of the 'great man'. While he waits for Rio, Torchie reminisces, regaling him with memories of 'the good old days'. The time he gave her infant daughter, Donna, a lily in the market to stop her crying. She describes the teenage Donna's pregnancy by an unknown father and her death in childbirth. Painful, painful memories. She makes the same journey she did then; pacing the room as she did then; watching from the window as she did then. Dialogue is repeated verbatim placing us right at the centre of events. As she flips between tenses it is almost impossible to distinguish past from present. She has spent a lifetime thinking about this, reconstructing and reliving the story, as if by doing so the outcome might be changed. She weaves Travis into her tale as if he were a participant, which ironically he was. It was Travis who raped the fourteen-year-old all those years ago and initiated the tragic sequence of events.

When Travis discovers he has importuned his own daughter his violent past finally catches up with him.

Torchie Well, perhaps it's best that you can't remember Donna. You'd be so upset if you knew what happened to her.

Pause.

It was terrible.

Pause.

I see a bruise.

A bruise on my Donna. But not a normal sort of bruise. Lor'struth, no. If I tell you where it was, Mr Flood, perhaps you can guess what kind of bruise it is.

She touches her neck.

It's here!

Slight pause.

A lovebite it is, Mr Flood. She's no longer the six-year-old girl you gave the lily to, Mr Flood. That was in the beginning of the heydays. No, we're at the end of the heydays now. Nineteen sixty-nine. And, although my Donna might still have her hair in a ponytail and smell of popcorn, she's fourteen years old. And she's standing in front of me – in this very room – with a lovebite on her neck. She's trying to hide it under her blouse collar . . . but there it is! 'Who did that, Donna?' I ask. She doesn't want to tell me. 'Is it someone at school . . . All right, all right! Don't get in a mood. Just make sure your dad doesn't see it. He'll hit the roof if he does and kill the boy to boot. And I hope you're not doing anything silly – Where are you going? Don't storm into the bedroom! I haven't finished with you yet!' But I don't pry any more, Mr Flood. I've got to allow her some privacy, haven't I? It's only a lovebite. No harm in it. I won't ask any more questions. It's the right thing to do, don't you think, Mr Flood? Tell me it's the right thing to do!

Slight pause.

It's a few months later now, Mr Flood. I'm waiting for my Donna to come home from school. Quarter past four. She should be here any minute. I start making tea. Half past four. She's probably chatting with a friend. She's very sociable. Five o'clock.

She starts pacing the room.

She's never been this late before, Mr Flood. Not without telling me. Lor'struth, she knows how I worry. I'm imagining all sorts of things.

She goes to window.

There's no sign of her, Mr Flood! 'Donna! Donna!' Half past five. I know something's wrong, Mr Flood. What shall I do? If I go out to look for her, she might come back while I'm out. Or, if there has been an accident, the police might come. I'm a nervous wreck . . . And then the door opens. 'Where have you been, you naughty girl! It's nearly six o'clock. I'm out of my mind with worry . . . What's wrong? . . . You went to see the doctor? But, why, Donna? What's wrong with you . . .' And what does she tell me, Mr Flood. What words come out of her mouth? I should have asked more questions when I saw the lovebite. 'Donna, you've got to tell me who the boy is . . . He's responsible. He's got to pay.' But she won't tell me, Mr Flood. She's crying. I stroke her hair. And all I'm thinking is, how am I going to tell Mr Sparks.

The Last Obit *by Peter Tinniswood*

In this one-woman tragi-comedy Millicent is a quirky, repressed spinster aged between mid-fifties and mid-seventies. As a child she was abused by her stepfather, an event that stalks the text. She was born in Liverpool (in my production it suited the actress to play her from Nottinghamshire but any northern accent will fit the cadences of the text). The play has a huge emotional range so there are lots of audition pieces for you in this one.

This is Millicent's last day as chief obituarist on *The Morning Telegraph*. She's been 'computerised' – replaced by technology. She sits in her dusty office writing her last obituary by hand. 'Dame Nina Plunkett, pioneer aviator and society hostess . . .', 'Dame Nina Plunkett, trades unionist and deputy head Naval Intelligence . . .' She relishes words, their shapes on the page, their sounds, their sensuality, 'insulting to churn them out mechanically'.

As Millicent roots through files of newspaper cuttings, life flashes before her in vivid snapshots. It is through these that her emotionally-starved nature is revealed.

In this 'snapshot', she remembers being taken as a young, impressionable girl to an exhibition of erotic art. After a slap-up high tea, H.K., her loathsome and married predecessor, takes her down an alley smelling of goat and introduces her to a heady world of wine, aromatic cigars and explicit sexual imagery. It's fairly clear what H.K. has in mind. But what impact does Eric Gill's erotica have on Millicent? Is she fascinated or repelled? What stirrings do they evoke? What painful memories do they trigger? When asked, her responses are non-committal, defensive. Yet it's funny that years later she remembers every lurid detail.

It is not until the end of the play we discover that the obituary Millicent is writing is her own; that Dame Nina is the personification of everything she would like to have been and the space she occupies, somewhere beyond the present.

Millicent 'Gill, Arthur Eric Rowton, sculptor, engraver, writer and typographer. Born Brighton 1882. Died 1940.' One long, lazy afternoon in late summer just before the outbreak of the Second World War H.K. sidled up to me and said in a whisper: 'Would you like to go out with me tonight?'

'Yes,' I said. 'Where to?'

'Somewhere special,' he said.

And it was somewhere special.

After work he took me to this café to have high tea. We had gammon, fried eggs, mushrooms, tomatoes, chips, hot toast and butter, scones, preserves and fancies.

The whole works.

Then he took me down this side street which smelled of goats. He knocked on the door of a shop with pictures in its windows. Later he told me it was a gallery. They let us in. There was a room full of pictures and sculptures and people smoking Turkish cigarettes and drinking wine from cardboard beakers.

'This, my dear, is Eric Gill,' he said.

'Who is?' I said. 'Can you point him out to me?'

He tut-tutted with his tongue.

'My dear, Eric Gill is not present in person. This is an exhibition of his work.'

'Oh,' I said. 'I see.'

We looked at the exhibition.

Well!

Talk about nudity.

Talk about pudenda.

Talk about being explicit.

There was this carving called *Ecstasy*. I'll always remember its name. There was this man and there was this woman and they were naked and they were standing up and they were doing it.

'What do you think?' said H.K.

I didn't reply.

He took me to another carving called *Votes for Women*.

I can see it now. To this very day I can see it vividly. There's this man and he's naked and he's stretched out on his back and there's this woman and she's naked, too, and she's sitting on him.

She's sitting between his legs and her knees are hunched up to her breasts and she's clasping him tightly round the waist and he's got his head tossed back and it looks as though he's about to thrash out with his legs.

What on earth are they doing I said to myself.

'Do you like it?' said H.K.

'Yes, it's jolly good,' I said.

The Lucky Ones *by Charlotte Eilenberg*

This play is about a pair of Jewish families living in Hampstead, the Blacks and the Mosenthals – refugees from Nazi Germany – and the impact their exile and displacement has on them and their children. They are 'the lucky ones' of the title.

Act One is set in 1968. Act Two is set in the present day.

In Act Two, Lisa Pendry is in her mid-sixties. She is the widow of an English academic and the daughter of a Berlin property owner who got rich by buying up cheap Jewish properties under the anti-Semitic laws before the war. She is intelligent, cultured, self-contained and still a stylish, attractive woman. Lisa has spent most of her adult life in England and her German accent has modified accordingly.

Back in 1968 Lisa bought a cottage in the New Forest from the Blacks and the Mosenthals, but Leo Black set an extraordinary condition on the sale. Perceiving her as 'a child of the generation that turned a blind eye' he demanded an apology for his family's suffering. Repudiating this second-generation guilt Lisa stormed out, but the incident forced her to see things differently and come to terms with some unpleasant realities. It also drew the two of them together and Lisa bought the cottage.

This scene is set on the day of Leo Black's funeral thirty years later. Lisa has returned to offer the cottage back to the family. Her story is quietly told and deeply felt, pre-emptive of the extraordinary gesture she is about to make. She presents herself as a German woman with a guilty conscience, trying to make amends for the sins of her father and assuage the shame and guilt she feels by association.

But there is a good deal more on her mind than that. Unknown to the family she's talking to, she has been Leo's mistress for the last thirty years. And she loved him. The cottage Lisa bought has been Leo's other home. What must she be feeling? She hasn't been able to attend Leo's funeral and for the first time in thirty years she is back in the garden where they first met. And she mustn't give anything away. Only a couple of well-placed pauses show a glimpse of what she is going through.

Lisa I – I have something to say which I think – I hope – may be of interest to you – to all of you. (*Pause.*) What was that play? There was a play, Büchner I think, and it begins; 'Gather round, small fry, and I'll tell you a tale . . .' I feel a bit like a character in that play, with you all looking at me . . .

Soon after I stormed out of here, I went to see my father in Berlin. I asked him what it had been like being a property developer in the 1930s in Berlin. '*Nicht so schlecht,*' he said. Not so bad. It was very awkward. You see . . . there wasn't this pervasive confessional atmosphere that there is today. What happened during the war was still not talked about. I tell you, when I was at college, there was a man with a strange limp, a Mr Schmidt always with a copy of Goethe in his pocket, and one day, instead of going straight into his lecture, he said that he wanted to tell us something, that he felt we should know. He told us that he, and many of his colleagues, had given their support to the youth rallies – not just once but on several occasions. At the time they'd really admired Hitler for his clear-mindedness, he said, and he remembered jostling with a load of others, a big crowd of them, all shouting, 'Heil Hitler.' 'I can't ask for your forgiveness but I ask you not to condemn me or my generation too harshly.' There was complete silence. It was a hot day, and I remember wanting to throw open a window and jump out. Eventually one chap said he felt nothing but horror for what he had heard. How could Mr Schmidt own up to something so shaming? How dare he talk to us about how we should judge him? A few others murmured their disapproval, and then one by one we just walked out. A week later, he handed in his resignation. And we all said quite right too – good riddance. We made a great show of our indignation – but it didn't feel – honest. I think we were all hiding our own sense of shame. (*Pause.*) Where was I? I can't quite believe that I'm back in the garden, telling you all this . . .

The point is that I was with Papa asking about the unaskable. I knew I was walking on eggshells but I went on. Had any of the properties he had bought at that time been from Jews forced to sell to him? Inside I was begging him to say no – but he couldn't. He just looked

118

– taken aback. He said maybe one or two, but he was working for a big company which made these decisions, he wasn't directly responsible for what they did, but he said it was '*eine sehr gute Zeit*', a profitable time, because there was so much on the market. He was peering at me over his glasses. There was something defiant and hurt about the way he was looking at me, how could his own daughter be putting him in this position? I couldn't hold his gaze. I turned away. He changed the subject – thank God, and . . .

When I came back to London there was a letter from Bruno, apologising for Leo's behaviour. I wrote back, straight away, and said I felt sorry too. Then Leo contacted me directly – would I still like to proceed. And I said yes. But, you see – I did pay for the cottage with money from my father, Leo was absolutely right. I have always thought it's never really belonged to me. How could it? It's part of your inheritance, not mine. And now that Leo is dead, I er . . . I'd like to return it to you both.

Here *by Michael Frayn*

This is a surreal play about how the choices we make conspire to change the 'here' and now.

Pat is in her sixties. She has been a widow for four years. She's lonely. While the death of her husband, Eric, has been a great release she is still preoccupied with the daily minutiae of their lives. There's not much left in hers. She has let an empty room at the top of her house to a young couple, Cath and Phil. But what if the future of the world hinges on where they place the bed or kitchen table? While the couple wrestle with this conundrum Pat can't help being the interfering landlady, making frequent visitations with chatty advice and unwanted furniture, like her late husband's chair.

In this speech Pat has settled down for a chat. She's sharing memories of her embattled marriage with Cath. It's woman to woman. Cath is having her own problems. She confides how she and Eric divided household responsibilities and apportioned blame. Everything Pat says about Eric has a pejorative edge. Hers was a marriage subsumed by trivia and festering grievance, where habits of blame and counter blame were the stuff of life. She re-enacts their petty exchanges, colouring Eric in with her feelings of frustration and resentment. Not a look, not a raised eyebrow, not a tone of voice has been forgotten. The broken sash, the doorknob, the washing machine, mirror the dysfunction of a relationship where communication was as broken as the washing machine and neither was prepared to take responsibility or give an inch. The marriage she describes is as empty as Eric's old chair.

Pat I was always the windows. Windows and door handles. And the roof. And the fireplaces. Because he liked modern, you see, Eric. He was always for modern. So anything that wasn't modern in the house, and it went wrong, that was my fault. He'd sit there reading his paper and I'd know something was up just from the look on his face. So I wouldn't say anything – I wouldn't give him the satisfaction. I'd wait. He'd go on reading the paper, not a word, just this tight little look, and I'd know he'd got this wonderful grievance. I'd wait. *He'd* wait. Then just as I was going out of the room, say, just as I was putting the supper on the table, out it would bounce. 'The bedroom door handle,' he'd say. It used to make me so cross! 'The bedroom door handle.' Like that. As soon as he said it I could feel my muscles all clench up. I'd just stop where I was, look at him, wait, not say anything. 'It's loose, it's going to come off,' he'd say. And so pleased with himself! Always knew I'd got a bad character, and now here I was, caught in the act, letting the bedroom door handle get loose. So of course I wouldn't admit it. Nothing to do with me! 'Oh,' I'd say, 'is it really? Then why don't you get upstairs and mend it?' But inside, Cath, inside, I knew he was right, I knew it was me that had done it, because if it was the door handle then it had to be me. So he wouldn't mend it, and I wouldn't get Mr Weeks to do it, and he'd sigh and raise his eyebrows every time he put his hand on it, and not say anything, and I'd look the other way, and not say anything, until in the end it'd fall off, and then at last, with a special holy look like Jesus picking up the cross, he'd get the toolbox out, and there wouldn't be any screws in the tin, so he'd have to do it with three nails and some glue instead, and there'd be blood dripping on the carpet, only he wouldn't let me put a plaster on it for him, and then I *couldn't* tell Mr Weeks about it when he came to do the boiler because that'd look as if I was criticising his handiwork and turning up my nose at the great sacrifice he'd made even though he was in the right and I was in the wrong.

Pause.

The boiler, that was me as well. The boiler, the drain outside the

122

back door. Yes, I don't know why I was the drain. But then *he* was the lights and the washing machine. Oh yes. All the machines, all the electrical. Anything modern, you see. He'd come home in the evening – darkness. 'That washing machine,' I'd say before he could so much as open his mouth. 'You'll have to do something about it, Eric. Water all over the floor. Flash! Crack! I wonder it didn't kill me.' And at once he'd go mad. 'There's nothing wrong with the machine,' he'd say. 'It's what you ask it to do.' Shouting away at me. Because he knew it was his fault, you see, the washing machine. If it was a gadget, if it was labour-saving, then that was his responsibility. Poor Eric. Poor old boy. But you can't take the blame for everything, can you, Cath. You've got to divide things up.

Rose *by Martin Sherman*

Rose is a play about memory where past and present are deeply interfused. It is a portrait of a 'survivor' – a strong intelligent woman whose feisty spirit and independent mind have been shaped by iconic events. It is a one-woman play and you should be able to find any number of audition pieces in it. I have chosen the speech at the beginning, which sets the tone and agenda.

Rose is an eighty-year-old Jew from a tiny Russian village, a survivor of the Warsaw ghetto who escaped by ship to Atlantic City to bring up her second family in America. We are just entering the new millennium, but Rose's roots are deep in the past and another culture. 'A world of chopped liver and dybbuks.' 'I stink of the last century, but what can I do?' she bemoans. She 'sits shiva' on a hard bench – a Jewish custom for remembering the dead. But who is she 'sitting shiva' for? She learns from the television that a nine-year-old Arab girl has been shot by her grandson, who has returned to Israel and is living as a settler on the Palestinian West Bank. Horrified by a world she doesn't understand and finds abominable she clings to membership of a race and culture that sustained her in the sewers of Warsaw after her own little daughter, Esther, was shot in front of her by a young Ukrainian soldier. She never mourned her properly. She was too busy staying alive. Now she can.

Rose's breathing is bad. Her own life is drawing to a close – a prospect she embraces. She remembers a long and remarkable life and struggles for a sense of belonging in a changing world.

———————————

Rose *sits on a wooden bench. She is eighty. There is a bottle of water and a glass on the bench, as well as a refrigerated pack. Occasional noise can be heard outside.*

Rose She laughed. And then she blew her nose. She had a cold. The bullet struck her forehead. It caught her in the middle of a thought. She was nine.

Pause.

I'm sitting shivah. You sit shivah for the dead.

Pause.

Shivah sounds like the name of a Hindu god. Maybe it is. I had a flirtation with Oriental religion once. I envied the true Buddhists; they were able to reincarnate; not like us – when we're dead, we're dead; this life, that's it – it's the Jewish curse, we don't have heaven or hell and we don't come back – it's now or never. Of course, for me, now is hardly here any more. I'm eighty years old. I find that unforgivable and suddenly it's a millennium and I stink of the past century, but what can I do? I'm inching towards dust, and sometimes I wish it would hurry, preferably in the middle of a thought, or a sentence, just like that, although not by a bullet to the forehead. And then I wonder if anyone will sit shivah for me; maybe in this bright new twenty-first century they won't sit shivah any more. Well, the ultra-Orthodox will, of course, but something like shivah, in reality, doesn't have much to do with religion, it's just Jewish. You sit on a wooden bench for a week, you laugh, cry, argue as you remember the dead, the particular dead of this particular shivah, and you eat a lot, and kvetch a lot, and you get a sore behind, and it reminds you that you belong to a people, a race, a culture of sore behinds and complainers and heated discussions, of minds in turmoil and minds in flight and minds exploding like the atom, which I still don't understand, but it changed the world, well, it changed the last century, the world that was, and Albert Einstein came from the same street in Germany as my second husband's cousin, what can I tell you? Maybe this past century will be in fact the next to last century, and will it all be because a restless people produce restless minds; when you don't belong anyplace, your mind doesn't belong anyplace, you're owned by no one, except God, and God is only an idea, and so if you believe in God, you have to believe in ideas; except now, who believes in God except the fanatically committed, and if that's true, who believes in ideas? Now is different, anyhow; we don't wander any more; we have a home.

Pause.

I can't catch my breath.

She tries to control her breath. Her problem is very quiet, almost unseen, but she can feel it. She pours a glass of water.

At my age, breathing is one of the few pleasures I have left.

Acknowledgements

All plays published by Methuen except where otherwise stated.

Any enquiries regarding performance rights should be made to the authors' agents as listed below.

p8 extract from *Dreams of Anne Frank* copyright © by Bernard Kops, 1997 c/o Sheil Land Associates Ltd., 43 Doughty Street, London WC1N 2LH.

p11 extract from *Cooking with Elvis* copyright © by Lee Hall, 2000, 2002, c/o Judy Daish Associates Ltd., 2 St Charles Place, London W10 6EG.

p13 extract from *Tokens of Affection* copyright © by Maureen Lawrence, 1991, c/o Broom Garth, 38 Ben Rhydding Road, LS29 8RL.

p15 extract from *Beached* copyright © by Kevin Hood, 1991, c/o Cruickshank Cazenove Ltd, 97 Old South Lambeth Road, London SW8 1XU.

p17 extract from *Joyriders* copyright © by Christina Reid, 1987, Alan Brodie Representation Ltd., 211 Piccadilly, London W1J 9HF.

p19 extract from *For Colored Girls Who Have Considered Suicide/When the Rainbow is Enuf* copyright © by Ntozake Shange c/o Russell and Volkenning Inc., 50 West 29th Street, New York, NY 10001, USA.

p23 extract from *Her Aching Heart* copyright © by Bryony Lavery 1991, The Peters, Fraser and Dunlop Group Ltd, Drury House, 34-43 Russell Street, London WC2B 5HA.

p26 extract from *Bloody Poetry* copyright © by Howard Brenton 1985, c/o Casarotto Ramsay & Associates Ltd., National House, 60-66 Wardour Street, London W1V 4ND.

132